Action Based
Communication

changing
experience
through
language

Renée Barnow

authorHOUSE®

AuthorHouse™
1663 Liberty Drive, Suite 200
Bloomington, IN 47403
www.authorhouse.com
Phone: 1-800-839-8640

First published by AuthorHouse 1/25/2008

ISBN: 978-1-4343-3563-0 (sc)

Printed in the United States of America
Bloomington, Indiana

This book is printed on acid-free paper.

Cover design inspired by Robbie Balan, Pulp Invitations, and executed by the author.
Interior designed by the author.
Illustrations conceived by the author and executed by Aimee Maescher, Nisse Designs.
Author photo by Violetta Manavis.

Contents

List of Figures

Dedication

For my Mom and the memory of my Dad. Both learned English after emigrating to the United States, and both taught me the value of attention and choice. I carry with me always their voices: Mom, I will forever hear telling me, "The tone makes the music" ("Der Ton Macht die Musik") in her native tongue; and Dad, whose favorite idiom was "keep a stiff upper chin."

As I considered the importance of language and how human beings interact with the world, it struck me that in many ways the development of language was like the discovery of fire—it was such an incredible primordial force. I had always thought that we used language to describe the world—now I was seeing that this is not the case. To the contrary, it is through language that we create the world, because it's nothing until we describe it. And when we describe it, we create distinctions that govern our actions. To put it another way, we do not describe the world we see, but we see the world we describe.

Joseph Jaworski

Acknowledgments

I have abundant appreciation and gratitude for my family and friends for listening to and playing with the material in Action Based Communication for many years. These people have been with me from the beginning.

Janice L. Nicholson, former associate vice president at Howard University, knew I would make a positive difference and made it possible for me to test the material with faculty, staff, and students. The opportunity supported making Action Based Communication come to life. Linda Mei Fang, School of Engineering, Temasek Polytechnic (Singapore), encouraged me to present a workshop on the basics of Action Based Communication for the institute's faculty. The experience enriched this book.

Humble thanks to John D. Carter, former CEO Gestalt Institute of Cleveland, and now President, Gestalt Organization & Systems Development Center, who at a class on leadership elegantly challenged me to rethink the "perfect" conditions for writing this book.

Several people reviewed drafts, some more than once. I am grateful to each for their encouragement, generous comments, insight, and suggestions throughout the writing process. Dost Deniz provided comments on an early draft, as did Yole

Patterson. Barbara Bey and Carol Goldsmith offered suggestions on subsequent drafts. Cheri Goldstein and Marlene Bellamy each read two versions: Cheri provided input on early drafts; Marlene, on later ones. Wendy Evans reviewed multiple versions at each stage of the book's development, and more.

For years Miriam Grogan offered to proofread the book once I was ready, and I appreciate her diligence and value her rigorousness in doing exactly that.

Anne Rubin offered the quiet and space I needed to work on this book, making her home in southern California available as a writing haven on several occasions. I am grateful for the physical and personal environment she provided in support of the creative process.

I shared my progress with a virtual support team, and after completing each draft they provided enthusiastic and encouraging messages. Special thanks to Lois Meredith who responded to each of my e-mail status updates. The team's words made writing this book more fun.

I learned from each person's contributions: their efforts made Action Based Communication more user friendly and helped mold this book into what it is.

Preface

As early as grade school, I was "teaching" the basics of Action Based Communication, or ABC. Back then I wasn't aware of the methods I was using. Years later I learned that my first grade teacher placed me strategically in the classroom, knowing that in a difficult situation or crisis I would talk and act calmly with classmates and lead them to a safe place.

My awareness of ABC's basics came into clearer focus starting in summer 1993. The federal government agency where I was one of 18 employees received a threat of termination. As the only non-attorney member of the professional staff, I was part of, yet separate from the organization. Faced with the possibility of being shut down, our interactions and behavior began to change. How were we changing? We were not as friendly toward each other and had lost our sense of humor and connection.

Once the initial threat seemed to have passed, we returned to more collegial ways. However, the next year the threat reappeared, and again our ability to connect as an organization became fragmented.

Congressional budget deliberations kept the agency on life support, which took its toll. When the organization was abolished in fall 1995, most of us were barely connected with ourselves, let alone with other staff members.

Wanting to understand what was happening, I looked at the area I knew best: verbal and nonverbal language. Were there specific, common words that we used in casual conversation that were different from ones we used before 1993? Was our body language different around the conference table during weekly staff meetings? Did language affect our ability to perform?

What I had learned about the value of attention and choice from my parents (see the Dedication, p. v) helped me answer the questions. Through the three-year transition to elimination, our verbal and nonverbal language reflected our mood. I noticed that we used more negative words and sat with our shoulders turned forward and down, whereas before we sat with our shoulders apart and back. Absenteeism increased.

Almost a decade later, in a conversation with one of the three top executives of the agency, he confirmed that, "The 1993-1995 period was the worst three years of my 30-plus year professional life."

Soon after the agency shut down, a former colleague who was then an associate vice president at a major university, asked me to provide consulting services. The specific assignment was to work in the highly charged atmosphere that resulted from a change in administration and help shift the environment to a positive one.

The timing of her call was perfect. I was excited about the opportunity to explore what I experienced at the small government agency in a large group setting. Soon after beginning the consultancy, I started formalizing my observations and experience into Action Based Communication™.

At the university, I was able to test the methodology on a diverse—in terms of culture, socioeconomic status, age group—population of faculty, staff, and students, for many of whom English was a second or third language. The university served as a living lab for the next two years.

After many years of being encouraged to document my instinctive, natural body of work, I set aside time to write this book. Only then did I begin reading about topics included in my own methodology. My reading confirmed the underlying principles and practices of *Action Based Communication: Changing Experience through Language*.

I learned that Action Based Communication is a one-of-a-kind blend, similar to a meritage wine, which is made from a variety of grapes.

As I was developing and delivering Action Based Communication, I was unconsciously integrating and incorporating some of the dynamics and principles from communication theory, mediation, kinesis, neuro-linguistic programming, neuroscience, physiology, and psychology. My lessons came from my own experience and from interviewing and practicing with people at the university and with clients, as well as with family and friends.

I witnessed the positive results of Action Based Communication in my coaching and consulting business. I know the program works.

Experience counts in Action Based Communication. Experience is convincing.

rb

Introduction

n important purpose of communication is connection. Action Based Communication™ (ABC) demonstrates, through the physical aspects of speaking and hearing, how single words and short phrases can make a big difference in the way we relate to others. Without this knowledge and full consciousness, our choices can result in connection or in disruption—a break in communication.

The message of this book is intended for mid-level managers, new leaders, new business owners or equity partners, sales staff, and people going through professional or personal transitions— those most likely to face situations where the potential for losing connection through poor communication is greatest.

The ABC methodology compares word usage to physical exercises, which is what differentiates the program from other work on communication. Action Based Communication offers word substitutions that support making connections, first with yourself and then with others. With more connections, you will have a better relationship with yourself and with other people— especially at work, personally, and as a member of a team.

Throughout the book, disruption and connection icons identify which words or phrases cause disruptions and which create connections.

Disruption and Connection

We use language to represent our experiences. By paying attention to the effects of language on experiences and mindfully choosing words—do they disrupt or do they connect—you can consciously improve outcomes and experiences.

If you want a different result, take a different action. The action is word choice.

Icons represent disruption and connection:

   Cause disruption

   Create connection

What ABC Means

Here is how the two parts of the book title relate.

- **Action Based Communication**—Acting out words, phrases, and concepts to experience their effect. This is done through a series of exercises, during which action helps people clarify the messages they send. Some of the action in the

  > Words may show a man's wit but actions his meaning.
  > Benjamin Franklin

  exercises involves clearly and slowly enunciating or sounding words out with the mouth, and exaggerating facial muscles. Movement of the lips and tongue causes physical sensations, forming a connection in the body to what is happening outside.

- **Changing Experience through Language**—Recognizing shifts in experiences that result from small changes in verbal and nonverbal language. Being aware of shifts helps people clarify messages or information they receive. Experiencing

  > . . . to do something successfully we need to be aware of what we are doing.
  > Colin McGinn

  different outcomes requires taking different actions. In ABC, the action is to substitute one word for another to produce a different experience.

How ABC Works

Simply substituting one word or phrase or adjusting the body ever-so-slightly can produce "aha" moments. Action Based Communication works through these word substitutions or body shifts. Although achieving the immediate experience of the moment might seem easy when doing the exercises, maintaining the new or different ways requires repeated and regular practice.

> *The seemingly simple act of 'paying attention' produces real and powerful physical changes in the brain.*
> Jeffrey Schwartz and Sharon Begley

Because practice is so important, approximately 25 percent of the book—the Language Reframing Log (Chapter 7)—is dedicated to monitoring and measuring your experience. By using the Log you will reinforce the relationship of attention and choice, as illustrated in Figure 1, the Attention-Clarity-Choice Cycle.

Figure 1: Attention-Clarity-Choice Cycle

About the Exercises

Through the exercises, you will experience how one small word or short phrase makes a big difference in creating a connection or causing a disruption. Enacting the words in the exercises makes the impact of word choice clear.

This icon introduces the exercises:

The Benefit of Practice

The same principle that applies to practicing a sport or a musical instrument or a dance routine applies to practicing the word and phrase substitutions in ABC. People learn Action Based Communication through kinesis (body movements) and repeated practice. Kinesthetic learning is the highest form, offering the greatest retention because we learn first and retain longest through the body—knowing in the bones or having muscle memory. With practice, choosing the words that create a connection will be easier and occur almost without thinking. Through repetition, you will understand and appreciate the effects of word substitution.

Repeated practice causes physical changes in the brain that result in new signals, new energy, and a new capacity to connect. The Action Based Communication methodology is built with communication as the structure for creating connections with yourself and then with others. The connections occur first in the brain.

Some people think that learning proceeds in a ladder-like or step-wise fashion. With practice you will move up the ladder, as illustrated.

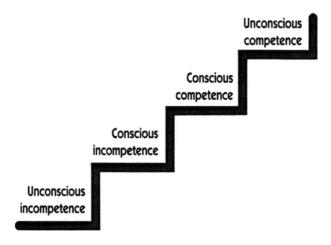

Figure 2: Maslow's Learning Ladder

When to Use ABC

Action Based Communication is useful as a general internal operating system and in many specific circumstances:

- Professional transitions
- Difficult situations at work
- Negotiations
- Sales presentations

- Group discussions of different opinions
- Strategic planning sessions
- Team meetings
- Customer relations
- Family discussions
- Personal relationships

Chapter 1: Laying the Foundation

anguage is the foundation that either supports connection or allows for disruption. Language represents sensations, feelings, thoughts, and perceptions. We communicate using many forms of language—art, body, color, dance, food, music, thought, and words. While the ways we use language

> *Thought is the most powerful action.*
> John D. Carter

vary, most of us communicate daily using both the language of thoughts and words and the language of the body.

Layers of Communication

In Action Based Communication, the layers of communication operate much like a skipping stone in a still pond or lake. The rippling effect moves from thoughts (internal dialogue) to words, either written or spoken (external dialogue), to the body (external language that is unspoken), as illustrated.

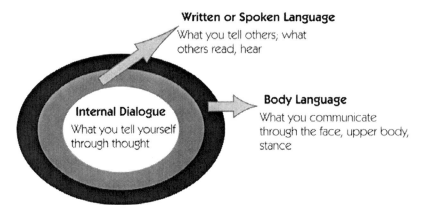

Figure 3: Communication Layers

Internal Dialogue

Messages begin from within, from our internal feelings and thoughts. Because human beings are born without language, we initially experience the world solely through our primary senses of sight, sound, touch, taste, and smell. As a result of learning to feel before learning to think, the dialogue of infants is only through feelings, most specifically the gut. Internal dialogue is essential and a prerequisite for engaging with others.

> *All conversations are with myself, and sometimes they involve other people.*
> Susan Scott

Speech and action are closely related. Words are tools: the very essence of action. We use them to abstract, discriminate, analyze, and dissect the world into pieces, objects, and categories. But speech is not only outer-directed;

within the self, words are the implements of thought. (Schlain, p. 21)

We communicate our feelings through actions and sounds, and receive messages through the same channels. With the development of language comes the capacity to think and communicate in words. Words express concepts. As adults, when we speak without thinking first, we are speaking from our innermost feelings.

Chapter 2 focuses on words used internally.

Written or Spoken Language

Messages move from internal thoughts and feelings to expression—words that we exchange with one another when writing or speaking. The Action Based Communication methodology compares word usage to physical exercises. Both choosing words carefully and engaging in physical exercise are important for daily living.

The media is replete with messages about the importance of physical exercise and the relationship of exercise to a positive attitude. Being in shape physically and mentally makes a person more effective, often affecting mood and behavior profoundly.

Similarly, words you use to communicate affect you and your reader or listener. As you write and speak, you read and hear your own words, and this sends messages to your own brain as well as to the brain of the person to whom you are addressing your words. Words expand or constrict thought processes as well as reflect the way we think. The way we think directly affects our bodies. Bodies react to words physiologically. A harsh word can release adrenalin and the need to fight or flee. A kind word can release serotonin, nature's own happy chemical. Words evoke images, sounds, and feelings.

> *A powerful agent is the right word. Whenever we come upon one of those intensely right words in a book or newspaper the resulting effect is physical as well as spiritual, and electrically prompt.*
> Mark Twain

Here the focus is on spoken language. In speaking and hearing, we need to pay attention to the voice, which communicates through tone, pace, and volume of delivering words, phrases, and sentences.

Chapters 3, 4, and 5 focus on words used externally.

Body Language

Body language communicates more strongly than written or spoken language. Eighty percent of communication is nonverbal. We learn first from what the body communicates; we remember best what the body experiences.

Facial expression is the most visible and accessible aspect of body language, with the eyes being the most reliable form of communication. As infants we begin communicating with and learning from facial expressions.

There are myriad facial expressions, each with its own nuance.

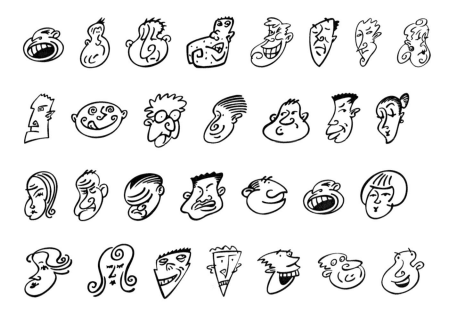

- Facial and body muscles reflect feelings
- Eyes, eyebrows, nose, cheek, and mouth offer a range of communication possibilities, and tell us much about personality
- The head, neck, shoulders, arms, hand, legs, and feet communicate as well

The diagram on the next page points out parts of the body. Each part sends a message. The physical space between the two people also tells us something.

Chapter 6 focuses on using unspoken external language.

Figure 4: Body Language

Male	Female
1 Head: slightly angled	9 Head: tilted
2 Shoulder (left): straight	10 Shoulder (left): raised slightly
3 Thumb (left): pointing up	11 Hip (left): straight
4 Neck: short, tucked in	12 Chin: jutting, leading
5 Elbow (right): slightly outward	13 Arms: crossed
6 Thigh (right): extended	14 Feet: turned in
7 Stance: a bit wider than hip width	15 Space between male and female
8 Foot (left): pointing out	

Body Language Experience

The purpose of this exercise is to become aware of how quickly you react to nonverbal messages.

- Imagine being in the presence of the male and female
- Focus on the image in Figure 4 closely for several seconds, only enough time to have an immediate reaction
- Use **one word** to record your first impression
- Describe briefly the physical sensation—what happened in your body—that accompanied your first impression
- Identify your feelings as you look at the picture

	Male	Female
First Impression		
	_____	_____
Physical Sensation		
	_____	_____
Identify Feelings		
	_____	_____

Summary

Internal, written or spoken, and body languages communicate with our brain as do the wordless languages of art, color, dance, food, and music. Regardless of the language used, we are constantly communicating, in one form or another, first with ourselves and then with others. We process external messages internally and take action as a result.

Chapter 2: Tools for Internal Dialogue

ools can build, disrupt, and destroy. In Action Based Communication, acronyms and mnemonic devices serve as shorthand for communication tools. Think of the devices as tools that help shape internal dialogue and simplify creating connections. A real life example (names have been changed and situations have been slightly altered) that demonstrates the benefit for selecting each tool is provided.

- Test DNA
- Maintain FIT-ness
- Listen to IT
- Rely on ME FIRST
- Value MOTH
- Don't SWEAT It
- Weigh Worry
- Practice WOW

Test DNA—Dissolve Negative Attitudes

Language and DNA are both codes, and we learn much from each. Language expresses the composition of feelings and thoughts. Similarly, in the world of medicine, DNA describes our unique genetic composition.

Genetic DNA is fixed, unlike ABC's *DNA*. Because Action Based Communication is about changing experience through language, by changing a single word or short phrase (the core of Action Based Communication) we can rewrite the code that sends messages to the brain.

As we learn in the next chapters, replacing one or two words can change a losing position to a winning attitude. Many of us naturally use "I can't _____" or "I don't _____" when another choice for saying the same thing is available.

Eduardo

Eduardo, the leader of a nine-member team, spends most of his time at work attending management meetings, leaving him little time to interact with his team. To help him keep track of on-going activities and decisions, Eduardo constantly tells himself, "**Don't** forget."

His days are long and Eduardo is exhausted from attending so many meetings. He often feels negatively about the work. In focusing on what he does **not** want to do, Eduardo constantly sends himself a negative message.

Eduardo also uses "**don't** forget" with his team members, who respond by saying, "I **won't**." More negative language.

Eduardo learned to shift his experience by replacing the negative message—"**don't** forget"—with a more positive message—"**remember**." **Positive messages are easier to respond to or act on than negative ones**. Eduardo also began using "**remember**" with team members, who responded with, "I will"—another positive phrase. Productivity increased, and the work atmosphere was more pleasant.

Repeatedly replacing the negative "**don't** forget" message with the more positive "**remember**" message helped Eduardo *dissolve negative attitudes*. Eduardo created the connection to what he wants to remember more easily, which then allowed him to manage his time more effectively.

Don't forget 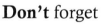   **Remember**

Here are additional examples that demonstrate the power of word choice to *dissolve negative attitudes*.

Habitual Response	Substitution
Don't be cruel	Love me tender
Don't be late	Be on time
Don't leave	Stay
Don't rush	Take your time
Don't take yourself seriously	Laugh at yourself
Don't wait	Act now

Are you aware of habitual responses you give that are negative? The exercise on the next page will help you to discover word substitutions you can use to *dissolve negative attitudes*, thus creating positive ones.

Choose *Dissolve Negative Attitudes*
Experience the Joy of Connection

Dissolve Negative Attitudes

- Note a few concerns you frequently voice to yourself.
- Write your habitual response to those concerns.
- Substitute positive responses for any negative habitual ones.

Concerns

1 _____

2 _____

3 _____

Habitual Response   **Substitution**

1 _____   _____

2 _____   _____

3 _____   _____

Maintain FIT-ness—Fun, Integrity, Tolerance

- **F—Fun** creates an environment and opportunity for connecting
- **I—Integrity** is acting in a "pure, clean" way without hurting others and helps create a positive connection
- **T—Tolerance** is respecting others' opinions, customs, culture, and beliefs, again making or creating a positive connection possible

In much the same way as staying fit physically promotes well-being, maintaining Action Based Communication's *FIT-ness* promotes the well-being of connection.

Sharon

Sharon and Sean were partners in a small clinic that provided specialized cosmetic surgery. After years of working together, having fun and taking care of people, Sean decided to leave the practice. Because the two-partner model had worked well, Sharon decided she only wanted to bring in one new partner to replace Sean.

When she interviewed prospects, Sharon focused on medical skills and experience and financial stability, in addition to the person's sense of humor and ease in engaging in conversation—"bedside manner." Of the 11 people she interviewed, Martin was the closest to her ideal partner. She thought he would be fun to work with and was easy to talk with, plus his experience and finances were impeccable.

Martin was short, and in talking about him to others, Sharon referred to him as "the midget," laughing each time she said so. While she was having fun, she was, as is so often the case, doing so at the direct expense of someone else. She was failing to maintain the integrity and tolerance aspects of *FIT-ness*. She was unable to create a connection. Using the label midget conditioned Sharon's experience, preventing her from seeing Martin as an equal. Only after she began referring to Martin by his name in conversations with others, rather than with the derogatory term midget, was Sharon able to offer him the partnership.

Are you maintaining *FIT-ness*? How can you tell?

- Pay attention to your internal dialogue. Notice if you use labels when referring to people.
- Pay attention to your feelings. Notice if there is a place in your body that feels uncomfortable.

Choose *Maintain FIT-ness*
Experience the Joy of Connection

Listen to IT—Intuition Talks

One of the oldest and most effective ways we communicate is through intuition. Each of us is born with intuition and develops it to differing degrees. To paraphrase the old E.F. Hutton brokerage commercial, Action Based Communication suggests, "When Intuition Talks, Listen."

What comes readily to mind when reading or hearing "IT" is information technology. In this common reference, IT refers to an *external* data gathering

> *Your intuition is your best friend, and intuition takes only a second.*
> Yogi Bhajan

and management tool. In Action Based Communication, *IT*, *intuition talks*, focuses on an *internal* data gathering and management tool. As such, ABC's *IT* is a superior information processor. Listen to your *IT* to create connections.

Matt

Matt was the newest member of an eight-person team working with business and technical staff to accept an essential new database that was replacing a 40-year-old one. The only orientation Matt received on his first day was an introduction to the other team members.

Based on the brief time he spent with each person, Matt knew instantly who would be supportive and who would be divisive.

In fact, he remarked to his escort, whom he immediately trusted, that one of the team members was "poison."

During his first two months on the team, the divisions between those who Matt sensed were supportive and those he sensed were divisive became clearer and clearer. Matt's instant assessment was accurate. Trained as an attorney, Matt understood the importance of evidence and recognizing patterns. He had all the evidence he needed from the first few seconds of an interaction.

Because Matt listened to his *IT* he knew with whom to interact to get the work done.

What can you do if you want to confirm a gut or intuitive reaction to your internal dialogue?

- Search for supporting evidence
- Look for a pattern

Choose *Listen to IT*
Experience the Joy of Connection

Rely on ME FIRST—More Energy from Integrating Responsibility, Sensitivity, Truth

Although the acronym *ME FIRST* might horrify you because it goes against all those painful lessons you probably learned as a child about not being selfish, you can create connections with others or "Get to We" using the *ME FIRST* tool.

People who take responsibility for their actions have more energy for connecting with others because they connect first with themselves. People who are sensitive to their own wants and needs have an easier time being sensitive to the wants and needs of others. People who know the truth about their own feelings, thoughts, and beliefs (i.e., do not deceive themselves), and act in accordance with them, sense when others tell the truth about their own feelings, thoughts, and beliefs, and act accordingly.

The essence of *ME FIRST* is the same as the standard required airline instruction to put on your own oxygen mask first before assisting others.

ME FIRST is about taking care of your intellectual, physical, and spiritual self. Although *ME FIRST* runs counter to the conventions of personal sacrifice that some people follow, the internal dialogue of "Rely on *ME FIRST*" is a prerequisite for creating connections.

Gerel

Gerel, whose husband traveled for work every week, all week, managed his in-home office while raising four children. On the business side, she took responsibility for keeping records and corresponding with customers. On the family side, she took responsibility for everything during the week. She believed others came first.

While she was concerned about the needs of the customers and her children, she was not satisfied in her ability to fully understand them. People who function from an "everyone else first" perspective often carry a hidden expectation that everyone else is coming from the same belief and that they do not need to take care of themselves because everyone else will.

Based on how she treated others, Gerel expected people to take care of her. Not surprisingly, she was disappointed when they did not. When she sought help on this issue, she learned that by taking responsibility for herself first, which required shifting her beliefs, her interactions were more satisfying.

Gerel opened herself up to being more sensitive to her own wants and desires, without the expectation that others would do anything in return. As a result, Gerel was also able to act in accordance with the truth of her feelings, thoughts, and beliefs. She experienced "we" from learning to "Rely on *ME FIRST*."

Choose *Rely on ME FIRST*
Experience the Joy of Connection

Value MOTH—Move on the Hour

MOTH is similar to *ME FIRST* because the *MOTH* tool helps you connect with yourself as a prerequisite for connecting with

 others. Both *MOTH* and *ME FIRST* are internal dialogues, which when practiced over time, become habitual, and create a clear path for connecting. *MOTH* is an easy way to get clear—get physical. Move.

Movement can be minimal.

> *Nothing happens until you move.*
> Albert Einstein

In the same way that a small word can make a big difference, a small movement or a brief break in activity can make a big difference. Movement opens up a path to creating a connection between the body and the brain. Staying in one position for more than an hour interrupts the flow of cranial and sacral fluids, which bathe the brain and spinal cord.

The shift in body position is changing experience, which can move you from being or staying stuck. In a 1986 edition of *Self*, Carolyn Jabs stated, "Taking the right kind of breaks from any job or problem helps you to faster solutions and finishes."

Barry

Barry was the director of proposal development at a large scientific corporation, and his work was often intense.

Barry retained me to train and coach his proposal development team. I used *MOTH* as a key method for increasing energy. During the training session, I invited the team to slowly and with awareness move their heads clockwise and then counter clockwise for a few rotations. Once the proposal team began writing, I encouraged them to take periodic walks either outdoors or in the building.

After a round of proposals during which Barry observed his team using *MOTH*, he reported that the team had more stamina and were more positive about their experiences. He and his team learned to "Value *MOTH*."

The fastest way to change experience is through physical activity.

What actions can you take to reinforce "Value *MOTH*" if you work at the computer for hours on end?

Away from the Computer

- Run in place
- Lie flat on the floor with your knees bent. Push down slowly and gently with your feet and lift your back up off the floor slowly in small increments, one vertebra at a time. Return each vertebra to the floor slowly in small increments. Repeat.
- Take a short walk outdoors
- Walk the halls

Seated at the Computer

- Push chair slightly back from the desk, and then do slow, careful neck rolls clockwise and then counterclockwise
- Shake your arms and wrists
- Massage each finger
- Rub the palms of your hands together
- Stretch your legs
- Flex your feet moving from heel to ball
- Take a series of deep breaths

Choose *Value MOTH*
Experience the Joy of Connection

Don't SWEAT It—Staying with Everyday Avoidance Tires

Action Based Communication's play on "Don't sweat it" conveys a similar sentiment to the popular phrase—there is little value in focusing on small stuff. Being overly concerned about the small stuff can get exhausting. So too, can focusing on avoidance rather than on action.

ABC's version of *SWEAT* It—*Staying With Everyday Avoidance Tires*—is more than procrastination. Action Based Communication's *SWEAT* is active avoidance of doing something important.

Kinesha

Kinesha is a well-respected coach who developed a breakthrough technique with an almost 100 percent success rate. One of her clients was amazed and delighted with the outcome and encouraged Kinesha to let the world know about the method. Unsure if the business community would accept the method, Kinesha continued beta testing it for two years.

While she kept saying she was satisfied with the status quo, she revealed to a few of her colleagues that she wanted to teach her method to other coaches. Yet, she did nothing to move forward. As she continued testing, Kinesha continued to *SWEAT* It—*Staying with Everyday Avoidance Tires*.

She formed an advisory board to help her launch her method. As a group they told her that her activities were not aligned with her wants. Over the months the advisory board met, Kinesha continued to *SWEAT* It. She worked closely with one advisory board member, and after the first two meetings, Kinesha canceled the next few scheduled sessions saying she had not completed her "assignment." When probed, she admitted she was avoiding doing the work.

The avoidance was depriving Kinesha of the energy required to create the connection she wanted, letting the world know about her method. When she was made fully aware of the effect of her avoidance, she was able to adopt Action Based Communication's *"Don't SWEAT It."* Kinesha learned the message behind the avoidance: She wanted to write a book about her method rather than teach her method directly to others.

Suggested Actions So You Don't SWEAT It —Staying with Everyday Avoidance Tires

- Record on paper those items you consider small stuff
  - Hide the paper from yourself
  - Burn the piece of paper
- Work with a coach to gain clarity about priorities

Recording a list and then hiding or destroying it is a physical and symbolic action that removes the small stuff from inside yourself and from your visual field. The action clears space mentally and energetically. Cleared space makes creating connection possible.

Working with a coach creates space for discovering if you are actively avoiding what you want.

Choose *Don't SWEAT It*
Experience the Joy of Connection

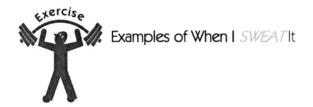

Examples of When I *SWEAT* It

In the space below note situations when you avoided doing what was important. These are times when **SWEAT** It was your prominent operating principle.

1 _____

2 _____

3 _____

4 _____

5 _____

Weigh Worry

Some people are constant worriers. You might know someone who seems to make worry a full-time occupation. Worrying is work, and as such requires energy and effort. Worry can also be a strategy to justify avoiding taking action.

With all the work involved in worrying, you might expect a change in outcome. Actually, outcomes remain unchanged.

Worry gets in people's way, often stopping them from taking action. As Dale Carnegie said in *How to Stop Worrying and Start Living* ". . . . worrying . . . . destroys our ability to concentrate." (p. 34)

Worry is an attempt to control the future on the basis of past experiences. Future orientation makes creating a connection in the present or taking action difficult. Worry has physical consequences such as ulcers and tension, and can hinder the ability to heal, hamper rational thinking, and shorten life, as in "he worried himself to death."

Worry without action is a choice. By controlling, reducing, or eliminating worry, people change their experience.

Consider the effect worrying has had on you. Pick an example of a recent worry you had. How did worrying affect you? What was the outcome?

If you **weigh worry** in the balance, **worry** will pull you down. To help you understand the effects of **worry**, think of and visualize **worry** as a "Lean/Lien on the Soul"—**weigh worry**.

Lean

Depending on the weight of an object that leans against you, you could get pushed over. To stay upright, you need to push against whatever is leaning on you. Pushing back can drain your energy.

With worry leaning on your soul, you are more likely to get pushed over and use up energy. Is this how you want to use your soul?

Lien

Many people have a lien on their personal property, such as their homes. If you default on the lien, some other entity could take away your home, your safe place.

Consider worry as a lien on your soul, the only personal property no one else can own. Is this how you want to use or perhaps lose your soul?

Instead, *weigh worry* as Bobby McFerrin did in his song "Don't Worry, Be Happy."

> *In every life we have some trouble*
> *But when you worry you make it double*
> *Don't worry, be happy.*

Staff at Federal Government Agency

This story is from my own history. When the staff of the federal government agency that I mentioned in the Preface received word that the agency would be terminated at the end of the fiscal year, focus gradually shifted from research to *worry*. Rather than spending time doing research for the agency and the greater public good, people spent increasing amounts of time actively engaged in *worry* about their personal futures.

With the new fiscal year in the fall, the agency received a reprieve, and the staff reengaged in research. As summer and federal budget deliberations rolled around, staff returned to actively engaging in *worry*. This pattern continued for several years.

Worry took its toll, robbing staff of the energy to search for and find satisfying positions. People spent so much time worrying that they were not aware of how *worry* affected them. If they had learned to *weigh worry*, they might have realized that the more they worried the worse their prospects became for seeking and finding future employment. *Worry* disrupted connecting with new positions.

Choose *Weigh Worry*
Experience the Joy of Connection

Weigh Worry Log

Complete the log and then assess how many of your worries were realized. Use the results to challenge yourself when you worry.

Worries	What Happened
_____	_____
_____	_____
_____	_____
_____	_____
_____	_____

Practice WOW—Worth of Work

Creating a connection sometimes requires work, and that work can take many forms. In physics, work is energy, and the result of expending energy or doing work is change. For some people, the work toward creating a connection could be paying attention to themselves and paying attention to others. For other people, the work could be in slowing down consciously and deliberately.

Me

Several times over a six-year period I had served one client, consulting on various programs. When asked to return for a third engagement, I hesitated because of the commute and the negative energy that resonated throughout the building. Although I reacted viscerally when I received the invitation, I chose to return for a variety of reasons. In making that choice I knew I had to support myself while doing the project.

Here is some of the work I did:

- Started work at 7AM, which was acceptable to the team lead and helped me miss some of the heavy traffic
- Took a longer than required route with fewer traffic lights that had a smoother flow

- Reframed how I thought about the time I spent sitting in stop-and-go traffic. Rather than thinking of the experience negatively as a waste of time, I considered the experience positively as private personal time.

Surviving in the negative environment required even more effort than the above steps to make the situation work effectively. I still did not feel a connection with myself, other consultants on the program, or with the work itself.

My solution was to work on changing my attitude. To help, I created the 12-step program, A^2—*Attitude Adjustment*, which appears after this box.

After developing and practicing the A^2 program, my energy shifted. I became an example for others for whom the negative energy of the physical structure interfered with their ability to work effectively. The work of shifting my attitude was well worth the effort. I created a connection with myself and with other people on the program.

Practicing the *Worth of Work*, *WOW*, in this case by shifting my attitude, was the key to changing my experience. To this day I carry with me a copy of my 12-step A^2 program.

A²—Attitude Adjustment 12-Step Program

1   Adopt "What is, is. What was, was." as a way of life

2   Keep the big picture in mind

3   Acknowledge and maintain a relationship with a spiritual entity

4   Slow down

5   Understand that each moment at the time is perfect

6   Think in smiles

7   Read or tell a joke, making sure to laugh at least once a day

8   Focus on and learn from others

9   Accept that I have needs

10   Ask for help

11   Express gratitude

12   Check in with myself and check out assumptions

Choose *Practice WOW*
Experience the Joy of Connection

Summary

Each of the acronym or mnemonic tools presented in this chapter provides a way to shape your interior dialogue.

- Pay attention to negative self-talk
- Be sure to honor your integrity
- Confirm your intuition
- Be sensitive to your own needs first
- Move part of your body every hour
- Notice the energy you spend avoiding forward going action
- Consider how worry affects you
- Engage in work you need to do to adjust to a difficult situation

By using the internal dialogue tools, you will build a structure for creating connections.

Chapter 3: Power Words

Now we shift the focus from words used in internal dialogue or thoughts to words used externally in written or spoken language. The emphasis is on spoken words and how the meaning depends on context. This is the first of three chapters on words used externally. In this chapter we discuss Power Words. Chapter 4 offers a set of words and phrases called Swing Words and Phrases, and Chapter 5 offers examples grouped as Throwaway Words.

Words are neutral, not good or bad. Yet, word substitutions can shift the situation away from causing a disruption toward creating a connection. For spoken language, in addition to the word itself, tone, volume, pacing, and content contribute to the disruption or connection.

While word substitution is a simple concept, the practice is difficult. Exercises are provided with each group of word choices to help you pay attention to and gain clarity from the experience. You will explore whether what you hear and what you see cause a disruption or create a connection.

The focus is on hearing rather than listening because hearing is a physical action that occurs in the ear. Listening is a social construct, and the action occurs in the brain.

Hearing	Listening
Physical	Social
Ear	Brain

The exercises require paying focused attention to how the words affect your feelings. Practice reinforces the Attention-Clarity-Choice Cycle (Figure 1) and is essential for changing behavior. You will experience how repeated practice in changing one word changes everything.

Summary of Power Word Choices	
Disruption	Connection
But	And
Intend, Plan	Will
Just	Exactly
No	Not Yet
Resolution	Commitment
To, At	With
Why	How, What

But/And

There is a world of difference between *but* and ***and***.

But

But sets up the condition for a turn or reversal in the idea previously presented.

Look 👁 at your mouth in a mirror to see what happens when you exaggerate and slowly enunciate saying *but*, using as many of the 44 facial muscles as possible.

Hear 👂 which sounds emanate when you say *but*.

Exaggeration is required so that you are aware of how you are using your facial muscles to enunciate.

The mouth moves down and the tongue (the heaviest muscle in the body) smacks against the teeth. Air is being forced through the teeth to make the "t" sound, which is almost like biting. Saying *but* severs action.

- *But* communicates stop
- *But* implies imbalance

> Your thought patterns are based on what you. . . . speak. . . . nerves in your mouth create the patterns of your brain function by the movements of your tongue.
>
> Yogi Bhajan

47

- ***But*** cuts

- ***But*** causes a disruption

Now pronounce a t. The tip of the tongue gets in the way of the airstream . . . . it stops it entirely. When the pressure builds up, you release the tip of the tongue, allowing the air to pop out . . . . What a listener hears when you produce a stop consonant is the following. First, nothing, as the air is dammed up behind the stoppage: stop consonants are the sounds of silence. (Pinker, p. 169)

Kick But or But Out

Avoid using ***but***, which brakes and breaks:

- Brakes (stops) forward going action. ***But*** can destroy a potential business transaction, derail labor negotiations, or silence family mediation.

- Breaks (severs) connections. ***But*** severs because it contradicts or denies what has gone on before. ***But*** can sever chances for gaining a prospective client.

And

And indicates a continuation of the same idea with new facts or presents various related thoughts. ***And*** connects because it joins clauses—the previous one and one that follows it.

Look 👁 at your mouth in a mirror to see what happens when you exaggerate saying ***and***.

Hear 👂 which sounds emanate when you say ***and***.

Exaggeration and slow enunciation are important. Both will help you see that your mouth moves up and your lips widen, as in a smile.

- ***And*** communicates ongoing action, forward movement
- ***And*** suggests balance
- ***And*** honors and respects individual differences
- ***And*** offers options
- ***And*** creates a connection

" . . . . [and] helps you to be curious, clear." (Stone et al, p. 43)

Use ***and*** to encourage working together, which is especially helpful during changing, uncertain, or chaotic situations.

Use the examples that follow to explore the world of difference when you substitute *and* for *but*. The first example is from language commonly used in television news reports. The second is from the draft of a book dedication.

Example 1

Local news broadcasts often lead off with a story about an accident and describe the victim's condition as either "stable **but** critical" or "critical **but** stable."

If you knew the person, which statement would you rather hear? Would you feel better if you heard critical **but** stable? Critical precedes *but*, which discounts the condition. Because stable follows *but*, you are more likely to hold on to the idea of the person's condition as stable.

Or, would you most like to hear that your friend is critical **and** stable?

The information that precedes *but* gets discounted and people usually remember the last word or phrase they hear. The last word or phrase "sounds" louder and has a greater impact.

Example 2

The author sent me the dedication that follows for comment and I shared my experience of reading *but*. I engaged the author in an exercise so she could have her own experience of hearing *but*, after which she substituted *and* for *but*.

Original book dedication: "To Michaela who thinks it's 'a hoot' *but* is very proud of having a mother in the third phase of her career, going into her fourth and most creative one."

Changed dedication: "To Michaela who thinks it's 'a hoot' *and* is very proud of having a mother in the third phase of her career, going into her fourth and most creative one."

- What happens to the information that follows *but* in the original?
- What happens to the same information when it follows *and* in the changed version?

Because the author wanted readers to grasp both the hoot and the pride, she decided to "kick but" or "but out."

Read out loud the sentences in Example 2 and you will hear a shift. *But* is an option breaker and a deal stopper; *but* discounts and can destroy the information that comes before it. *And* provides options; by

> *Words are the most powerful drug used by mankind.*
> Rudyard Kipling

definition *and* is a connector. Replacing *but* with *and* changes one's experience and how someone is heard.

Although sometimes it is appropriate to use *but*, the focus here is on making connections. Sometimes choosing to use *but* can be strategic and create precisely the experience you want.

 There could be occasions where substituting *and* for *but* is not appropriate. Sometimes *but* is precisely the word that best communicates.

When you want to connect, choose the more intimate power word *and*. Of the words included in Action Based Communication, *and* is the most important. *And* multiplies rather than adds connections. *And* is the sine qua non of connection.

Sami

Sami had a reputation as an engaged listener, which was one of the key factors in his rapid advance and promotion to team leader. His new team had several ongoing conflicts and disagreed about methodological approaches to its work.

Sami's first performance appraisal as a team leader began with his boss Victor saying how much the organization valued Sami's ability to offer different approaches and provide a "breath of fresh air." The discussion moved to how Sami worked with conflicts among team members. Victor offered the following, "You listen well to each member's individual concerns, *but* you allow the disagreements and dissension to continue." Sami heard the word *but* as a negation of the first half of the sentence. The last thing Sami took in was the criticism implied in *but*. He left the appraisal feeling that his listening skills were discounted.

Choose the power word *and*
Experience the Joy of Connection

Use *And* to Avoid Braking/ Breaking Options

Work with a partner to experience looking at and hearing each other first say *but* and then say *and*. **Exaggerate** and enunciate the words as you say them **out loud**, **slowly** to hear and feel the shift. Do the exercise looking into a mirror if you do not have a partner.

But
Say *but*
- Observe and feel lip position and movement
  - Describe physical experience—what happened?
- Listen for sound
- Name physical sensation
- Identify your feelings

Repeat

And
Say *and*
- Observe and feel lip position and movement
  - Describe physical experience—what happened?
- Listen for sound
- Name physical sensation
- Identify your feelings

Repeat

Record your answers on the log on the next page.

But/And Exercise Log: Lip Position and Movement, Sound, Sensation, Feelings

	But	And
Describe Lip Position and Movement	_____	_____
	_____	_____
Describe Sound You Hear	_____	_____
	_____	_____
Name Physical Sensation	_____	_____
	_____	_____
Identify Feelings	_____	_____
	_____	_____

Intend, Plan/Will

The difference between *intend*, *plan* and *will* is similar to the difference between "drawing a line in the sand" and "putting a stake in the ground."

People use "drawing a line in the sand" to suggest testing a position—a slight breeze could shift the line. "Putting a stake in the ground" is made as a firm declaration about a position or action. Biologically, sand does not support growth as well as the earth does.

> . . . . intending is not the *same* as willing,
> since willing is part of action while intending
> is preparatory and antecedent to it.
> (McGinn, p. 132)

Playing with the adage, "The road to hell is paved with good intentions," if you want to get to heaven, use *will*.

> In musical keys as in speeding tickets, it is the observed action, not the intention that counts.
>
> Daniel J. Levitin

Plan and *intend* are closely related. Like *intend*, *plan* is future focused without any commitment or guarantee that action results. As was the case for worry, future orientation makes creating a connection in the present and taking action difficult.

$$Intend + plan = 0$$

Record some of your recent intentions and plans in the following spaces.

My Recent Intentions

1 _____

2 _____

3 _____

4 _____

My Recent Plans

1 _____

2 _____

3 _____

4 _____

What did you notice about the language you used? What happened as a result of your intentions or plans?

Intend, Plan

Intend does not produce results. Neither does *plan*. When someone tells you that he or she *intends* to do something, how sure are you that that person will follow through? What if someone tells you that he or she *plans* to do something? What is your expectation? *Intend* and *plan* are both future oriented.

Examples

- I *intend* to complete the assessments by the end of the month.
- I *plan* to complete the assessments by the end of the month.
- I *intend* to organize the files before I begin writing the report.
- I *plan* to organize the files before I begin writing the report.

How confident are you that you will complete the assessments by the end of the month? How confident are you that you will organize the files before you begin writing the report?

Both *intend* and *plan* require the word "to" to complete the thought. In these cases, "to" gets in the way of creating a connection.

Many of us know the statement, "Good intentions are often unrealized." The same is true for plans. Yet, Action Plans see results. The word "action" makes the difference.

Will

Will delivers outcomes. There is power in *will* because action results. When you tell someone you *will* do something, the

> For purposes of action nothing is more useful than narrowness of thought combined with energy of will.
> Henri Frederic Amiel

other person has an expectation followed by evidence that you delivered on your promise. *Will* carries accountability.

What do you notice in the examples when *will* replaces *intend* and *plan*?

Examples

- I *will* complete the assessments by the end of the month.
- I *will* organize the files before I begin writing the report.

Will is a direct connection. *Will* is where the action is. There is power in *will* power.

> Work usually follows will.
> Louis Pasteur

The role of the will is not to understand the world but to change it . . . the will is by nature active . . . The will effects changes by virtue of

its embodiment: to bring about material changes
the will must be linked with bodily actions capable
of working those changes. (McGinn, p. 117)

Helen Marie

In the first meeting of a task force to survey training delivery,
task force head Helen Marie told members, "I *intend* for this
group to explore various data collection methods."

Task force members lacked enthusiasm for their participation
and were not sure what the cause was. Helen Marie sensed this,
and asked her supervisor, who was at the initial meeting, for
advice.

In an effort to support Helen Marie, her supervisor suggested
substituting *will* for *intend*. In the next meeting with task force
members, when Helen Marie stated, "We *will* explore various
data collection methods," she sensed the team had more
energy. She noticed that she spoke more confidently. She
created a connection with herself and with task force members.

Choose the power word *will*
Experience the Joy of Connection

Create "Will Do" Activities: Experience Results

In this exercise you will take and measure action to test changing your experience through language.

For "To Do" List makers ("**to do**" is akin to *intend* and *plan*)

- Change the language from "To Do" List to "Will Do" Activities for the next three weeks.
- Check out and note your feelings as you check off the activities.

Some people do not hold themselves accountable to their "To Do" lists. Did you accomplish more with "Will Do" Activities than with a "To Do" List?

For non-"To Do" List makers

- Write a "Will Do" Activities sheet once a week for each of the next three weeks.
- Check out and note your feelings as you check off the activities.

If you are not a list maker, and you experimented with this exercise, did you accomplish more than you have in the past using "Will Do"?

Report your experiences on the log on the next page.

To Do/ *Will Do* Exercise Log

	To Do List	Will Do Activities
Item 1— Experience	_____ _____	_____ _____
Item 2— Experience	_____ _____	_____ _____
Item 3— Experience	_____ _____	_____ _____
Item 4— Experience	_____ _____	_____ _____

Just/Exactly

Casual conversation is peppered with the word *just*. *Just* carries a negative connotation, minimizing both the speaker and the receiver. We could save time and perhaps a business deal by communicating more positively using a modifier such as exactly, immediately, only, or precisely. Here we explore replacing *just* with **exactly**.

Example

Marcella and Cynthia are colleagues.

Marcella: "Cynthia, what a great idea to hold a slogan contest."
Cynthia: "Oh, it was *just* something that popped up."

What immediate physical reaction do you have to reading *just* in the example?

- Imagine Cynthia's tone of voice
- Pay attention to your feet, gut, upper body, and face

When hearing *just*, people usually feel their backs pushed up against a wall. The back and shoulders literally get tense. Upon hearing the word *just*, the body reacts to the denial and minimization by tensing and getting smaller.

By using *just*, Cynthia belittled herself and disrupted the connection with Marcella. Cynthia's minimization implies that Marcella's enthusiasm is wrong. Cynthia cut off Marcella's implied support and cut herself off from receiving a compliment.

Just

Imagine hearing, "We have *just* one month to secure the deal." When faced with deadlines people jump to *just* to define how much time is available to complete work. What is the unspoken message you hear?

People often hear *just* as almost a dare to meet the deadline and that there is some implicit punishment if they fail.

- *Just* describes a deficit
- *Just* diminishes
- *Just* truncates time
- *Just* denies

Exactly

Imagine being told, "We have *exactly* one month to secure the deal."

What immediate physical reaction do you have to reading *exactly*? What happens in your body?

- Imagine the speaker's tone of voice
- Pay attention to your feet, gut, upper body, and face

What is the unspoken message you hear?

People usually hear *exactly* as a call to action. As a result, they sit up straighter, placing both feet on the floor.

People use *just* to measure time and assets. Using *exactly* to measure time and eliminating *just* when measuring assets creates a connection.

Phil and Diana

As Phil and Diana's neighbor, I knew about their transition as a couple from practicing law to developing screenplays, including how their energies were shifting to marketing scripts to TV and film companies.

To accommodate their transition, they developed a new business plan and revised the one for their legal practice. Phil shared his concern that they had devoted *just* 15 hours per week to writing. Diana offered that after two years they had completed *just* one script. The 15-hour per week plan allowed them to continue earning an income while writing screenplays.

I asked Phil to replace *just* with **exactly** in describing the number of hours spent each week working on screenplays. In inquiring about how he felt after making the exchange, he told me he felt better and was punishing himself less.

I asked Diana to eliminate *just* when talking about the completed script. She reported feeling accomplished rather than apologetic in stating, "We completed one script in the past two years."

Choose the power word *exactly* or lose *just*
Experience the Joy of Connection

Use Exactly to Create Connections

Work with a partner to experience hearing each other first say *just* and then say *exactly*. Hear and feel the shift when you move from *just* to *exactly*. Do the exercise looking into a full-length mirror if you do not have a partner.

Just
Say *just*

- Describe the physical experience—what happens to your shoulders, back, and feet?
- Identify your feelings

Exactly
Say *exactly*

- Describe the physical experience—what happens to your shoulders, back, and feet?
- Identify your feelings

Record your answers on the log on the next page.

Just/Exactly Exercise Log: Shoulders, Back, Feet

	Just	Exactly
Physical Experience— Shoulders	_____	_____
	_____	_____
Physical Experience— Back	_____	_____
	_____	_____
Physical Experience— Feet	_____	_____
	_____	_____
Identify Feelings		
	_____	_____
	_____	_____

No/Not Yet

How do you answer questions inquiring about progress or status on projects? When asked about status, most people respond with yes or *no*.

Example

- Have you registered for the required training course? *No*
- Have you registered for the required training course? Yes

No

When people think about progress they tend to focus on the goal rather than the process. Focusing on the goal is important. However, focusing solely on the goal often results in using *no* when questioned about results. In that way, people diminish their efforts toward reaching the goal by restricting their response to a bald yes or *no* and stating *no*.

When you exaggerate saying *no* your lips come together in a point, forming a tight, closed circle with "o". This action closes out possibilities. The point is like a period that says stop.

No declares that the status is static.

When people answer *no*, they are saying moving forward, having options, or creating a connection is not possible. They cause a disruption and really are saying stop.

Not yet states that the status is fluid. *Not yet* pulls toward meeting a goal. Expand your choices of yes and *no* to include *not yet*.

Example

- Have you registered for the required training course? *Not yet*.

Not yet

Often we do not really mean *no*, rather we mean *not yet*. While the difference is subtle, there is a powerful shift in attitude and experience that results when you start replacing *no* with *not yet*.

What is your experience with the difference when you read the following example?

Example

- Have you found a new position? *No*.
- Have you found a new position? *Not yet*.

No suggests that you *will not* find a new position. *Not yet* says options and possibilities exist. *Not yet* suggests you *will* find a new position, create a connection.

Think of *yet* as an almost **yes**.

Look 👁 at your mouth in a mirror when you exaggerate saying *yet*.

Hear 👂 which sounds emanate when you exaggerate saying *yet*.

With exaggeration you will see that your mouth moves up and your lips widen as in a smile.

Getting to Yet

While making the change from *no* to *not yet* is not always appropriate, you would be surprised at how frequently you can make the switch.

By replacing *no* with *not yet*, you will begin experiencing a powerful shift in attitude.

Vijay

In the competitive commercial real estate market, Vijay was known as a super leasing agent, able to meet 90+ percent occupany rates under even the most difficult economic conditions.

Fellow agents in his firm were curious how Vijay managed to secure highly sought after tenants. Each used the same marketing protocols and followed the same sales techniques.

Unable to determine what Vijay did differently, the agents asked him for his secret. He invited them to listen to his language at the weekly sales meetings. During a particularly down market, Vijay, in response to questions about renting certain properties stated, "I have *not yet* rented the renovated building." When asked about renting their respective properties, other agents said, "*No*, I have not rented it."

Still curious, his colleagues wondered what difference there was between *not yet* and *no*. Vijay explained that when he said *not yet* he felt he would soon secure a lease. The *not yet* kept him moving forward. By saying *no*, Vijay's colleagues sent themselves a message that they would not be successful.

Choose the power words *not yet*
Experience the Joy of Connection

Work with a partner to experience looking at and hearing each other first say *no* and then say *not yet*. **Exaggerate** and enunciate the words as you say them **out loud**, **slowly** to hear and feel the shift. Do the exercise looking into a mirror if you do not have a partner.

No
Say *no*

- Observe and feel lip position and movement
  - Describe physical experience—what happened?
- Listen for sound
- Name physical sensation
- Identify your feelings

Repeat

Not Yet
Say *not yet*

- Observe and feel lip position and movement
  - Describe physical experience—what happened?
- Listen for sound
- Name physical sensation
- Identify your feelings

Repeat

Record your answers on the log on the next page.

No/*Not Yet* Exercise Log: Lip Position and Movement, Sound, Sensation, Feelings

	No	Not Yet
Describe Lip Position and Movement	_____ _____	_____ _____
Describe Sound You Hear	_____ _____	_____ _____
Name Physical Sensation	_____ _____	_____ _____
Identify Feelings	_____ _____	_____ _____

Resolution/Commitment

Do you make New Year's *resolutions*? If yes, how well do you keep them? Do you find yourself breaking your *resolutions* before June? Do you find yourself recycling *resolutions* from year to year? If yes, word choice may be a contributing factor.

Resolution

A *resolution* solves a problem. A *resolution* is in response to a deficit.

Examples

- My *resolution* is to lose weight
- My *resolution* is to listen better

Resolution repels or pushes against a problem. Even though the sentiments in the examples are positive, the underlying message is negative. The examples imply that the speaker weighs too much or does not listen well. *Resolution* causes a disruption.

Commitment

How would your experience be different if you made New Year's *commitments*? How do you think you would feel checking the progress of *commitments* mid-year versus checking *resolutions* mid-year?

For example, the field of mediation, as lawyers or mental health professionals practice it, engages disputants in making a *commitment* to an agreement. The disputants each contribute to the agreement that both parties sign.

> Until one is committed, there is hesitancy, the chance to draw back, always ineffectiveness. Concerning all acts of initiative (and creation), there is one elementary truth the ignorance of which kills countless ideas and splendid plans: that the moment one definitely commits oneself, then providence moves too.
> Johann Wolfgang Van Goethe

Through the communication lens, the choice of words used in this written agreement promotes moving forward.

As in recycling New Year's *resolutions* year after year, do you ever encounter the same difficulty repeatedly?

How might you face the difficulty if you made a *commitment* to do so rather than a *resolution*? Are you more likely to honor a *commitment* than a *resolution*?

Commitment attracts or pulls toward outcomes. People make commitments to do something, take action. *Commitment* creates a connection.

Leonard and Ralph

Ralph and Leonard, next door neighbors, shared more than their common property line. They shared unspoken annoyance about the height of utility lines on each other's property, among other issues. To resolve the low hanging lines, each called the respective provider. However, only Leonard could resolve one of Ralph's concerns—the fence that Leonard let fall into disrepair. After multiple requests to Leonard for a *resolution*, the fence remained in disrepair.

Ralph talked with me about how he could get through to Leonard. I suggested in each conversation he ask Leonard for a *commitment* to repair the fence. This seemed to work. Leonard responded that he would repair the fence next year when he had exterior work done on the house. Eight months later, the fence was repaired.

Resolution resulted in frustration; *commitment* produced results.

Choose the power word *commitment*
Experience the Joy of Connection

Write New Year's Commitments: Increase Possibilities for Successful Outcomes

In this exercise you will take and measure action to test changing your experience through language.

For New Year's Resolutions makers

- Make a copy of your New Year's *Resolutions*.
- Change the language from New Year's *Resolutions* to New Year's *Commitments* for the *resolutions* you made this year, regardless of today's date.
- Check your progress meeting the *resolutions* on the original and the *commitments* on the copy every three months.
- Note your feelings
- Write New Year's *Commitments* in early January next year.

For non-New Year's Resolutions makers

- Write New Year's *Commitments* regardless of today's date.
- Check your progress meeting the *commitments* every three months.
- Note your feelings.
- Write New Year's *Commitments* in early January next year.

Record your experience on the log on the next page.

Resolution/*Commitment* Exercise Log

	Resolution	Commitment
Item 1— Experience	_____	_____
	_____	_____
Item 2— Experience	_____	_____
	_____	_____
Item 3— Experience	_____	_____
	_____	_____
Item 4— Experience	_____	_____
	_____	_____

To, At/With

Are you the kind of person who talks *to* people, *at* people, or *with* people?

Reflect on times when a peer or partner has said, "I want to talk *to* you." What happened in your body? What feelings came up? Recall when you thought someone was talking *at* you. What happened in your body? How did you feel? What about when you hear, "I want to talk *with* you? How did your body react? How did you feel? To help recall what happened in your body, visualize now what happens to your body posture when you are being talked *to*, *at*, or *with*?

To and *at* suggest inequality and cause disruptions; *with* creates connections.

To

Look 👁 at your mouth in a mirror to see what happens when you exaggerate and slowly enunciate saying *to*.

Hear 👂 which sounds emanate when you say *to*.

When you exaggerate saying *to* the same physical formation occurs as when you exaggerate saying *no*. The lips form a tight, closed circle with "o". This action closes out others.

Ask someone to exaggerate and slowly enunciate saying *to* and observe his or her lips. They come together as a closed circle. Hear what you sound like when you say *to*. Hear what another person sounds like when he or she says *to*. You will hear something that sounds a bit abrupt. *To* causes a disruption.

At

Look ◉ at your mouth in a mirror to see what happens when you exaggerate and slowly enunciate saying *at*.

Hear 𝕕 which sounds emanate when you say *at*.

When you exaggerate saying *at* the same physical formation occurs as when you exaggerate saying *but*. Feel your tongue smack against your teeth.

Ask someone to exaggerate and slowly enunciate saying *at* and listen to the final sound. *At* sounds stop, and as the icons illustrate, communicates an inequality in position.

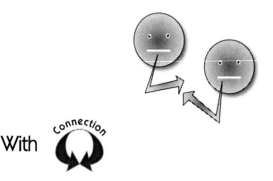

With

With is similar to *and*, suggesting balance and partnership. *With* creates connections.

Look 👁 at your mouth in a mirror to see what happens when you exaggerate and slowly enunciate saying *with*.

Hear 👂 which sounds emanate when you say *with*.

Feel your mouth move up.

Ask someone to exaggerate and slowly enunciate saying *with* and observe that person's lips expanding. As with *and*, you may find yourself smiling and seeing the other person smile as well. Speaking *with* and working *with* communicate equality and create a connection.

Using *with* when you are engaged in conversation creates a connection.

Remember to listen to the tone of voice when you hear *to*, *at*, and *with*. How do you take in each word? Notice where in your body each word lands.

Let's look at how seating arrangements reinforce *to* and *with* as disruptions and connections.

Figure 5: To and With Seating Formations

Choosing to use *to* can be strategic and create precisely the experience you want. As illustrated in Figure 5, there is more space between people when one uses *to*. *To* is directive.

In the diagram, the people who use *with* are physically closer to one another, making connection easier. When you want to connect, choose the power word *with*, which is intimate.

More about Sami

We met Sami, who provided a "breath of fresh air," on page 52. When he was promoted to senior team leader he inherited a team. What did his staff hear, feel, and think about being members of his team?

At weekly staff meetings Sami asked people to share their respective project status *with* one another. When he went to a person's cube, Sami said, "I want to talk *with* you."

Sami's staff heard *with* as a connection. Each member felt as if he or she mattered as an individual and thought that Sami believed each person was a valuable member of the team.

As a senior team leader, Sami talked *with* his direct supports. He operated from a position in which he worked *with* his direct reports rather than from a position in which his direct reports worked for him.

Choose the power word *with*
Experience the Joy of Connection

Work with a partner to experience looking at and hearing each other first say *to* and then say *with*. **Exaggerate** and enunciate the words as you say them **out loud**, **slowly** to hear and feel the shift. Do the exercise looking into a mirror if you do not have a partner.

To
Say *to*
- Observe and feel lip position and movement
  - Describe physical experience—what happened?
- Listen for sound
- Name physical sensation
- Identify your feelings

Repeat

With
Say *with*
- Observe and feel lip position and movement
  - Describe physical experience—what happened?
- Listen for sound
- Name physical sensation
- Identify your feelings

Repeat

Record your answers on the log on the next page.

To/*With* Exercise Log: Lip Position and Movement, Sound, Sensation, Feelings

	To	With
Describe Lip Position and Movement		
Describe Sound You Hear		
Name Physical Sensation		
Identify Feelings		

Use With to Create Connections: Activity II

Work with a partner to experience looking at and hearing each other first say *at* and then say **with**. **Exaggerate** and enunciate the words as you say them **out loud**, **slowly** to hear and feel the shift. Do the exercise looking into a mirror if you do not have a partner.

At
Say *at*

- Observe and feel lip position and movement
    o Describe physical experience—what happened?
- Listen for sound
- Name physical sensation
- Identify your feelings

Repeat

With
Say *with*

- Observe and feel lip position and movement
    o Describe physical experience—what happened?
- Listen for sound
- Name physical sensation
- Identify your feelings

Repeat

Record your answers on the log on the next page.

At/ *With* Exercise Log: Lip Position and Movement, Sound, Sensation, Feelings

	At	With
Describe Lip Position and Movement	_____	_____
	_____	_____
Describe Sound You Hear	_____	_____
	_____	_____
Name Physical Sensation	_____	_____
	_____	_____
Identify Feelings	_____	_____
	_____	_____

Why/What, How

Do you tend to ask questions starting with *why*? If yes, what kinds of responses do you get? *How* do people react to questions you ask that start with *why*? *What* happens? *How* do you respond or react when you are asked questions that start with *why*?

Why

- *Why* questions put people on the defensive
- *Why* questions create distance and push people away
- *Why* questions generate aloofness
- *Why* questions cause a disruption

Why often pushes people in the same way people feel pushed up against a wall when working against a deadline (as described in *just*). Questions that begin with *why* tend to be directed at a person, seeking answers about human behavior. Questions that begin with *why* tend to be experienced as a challenge.

Why is a generic challenge versus the specificity of questions that begin with *what* or *how*. Questions that begin with *what* or *how* tend to seek answers about observable behavior.

How/What

To learn more about an issue, a reaction (scientific or emotional), and to get to the truth of a matter, ask *how* and *what* questions.

In mediation, the focus is on *how* and *what* people need to agree on to move forward. In science, the focus is on questioning *what* happens and *how* that "what" occurred in either the controlled environment of a lab or in the universe.

> "Ask *How* rather than *Why* questions. *How* questions will get you an understanding of the structure of a problem. *Why* questions are likely to get you justifications and reasons without changing anything." (Linden, p. 5; capitalization in original; bold and italics are mine)

> "*What?* leads to information about nouns and pronouns. *How?* tends to directionalize the person's thinking toward the process, which is ongoing, dynamic, and changing." (Linden, p.235; italics in original; bold is mine)

- Response to *why* = Defensiveness
- Response to *how*, *what* = Engagement

To create a connection, use the more strategic *how* and *what*; avoid *why* questions.

 Listen to the speaker's tone of voice when you hear *why*.

Albert

When Albert asked his staff, "*Why* is the work going the way it is?" he was unsatisfied with the information he received and the lack of engagement with his staff. People found themselves stumbling to respond to his question and instead got stuck on the hidden statement that the way the work was going was unsatisfactory. *Why* evoked defensiveness.

Albert requested input about his style of asking questions and learned that his staff were put off, felt distanced, and sensed that they were being accused with his *why* questions. Albert's *why* questions disrupted any sense of engagement.

When he shifted to asking, "*What* is going on with the work?" or "*How* is the work going?" he was satisfied with the information he received. After awhile, he also noticed that his voice didn't crack the way it did when he asked *why* questions. Albert's experience changed as did the experiences of his staff when he asked *what* and *how* questions. *What* and *how* created a connection.

Choose the power words *how* and *what*
Experience the Joy of Connection

Get Muscle Definition with What **and** How

Why Questions

- Ask a colleague or friend *why* something happened.
  Why did _____ happen?
- Observe the person's body language when he or she responds.
- Pay attention to the person's tone of voice.
- Listen to the spoken language used in the response.
  o Which words does the person use? Are they defensive or charged?

How/What Questions

- Ask a colleague or friend *what* happened or *how* something happened.
  How did _____ happen?
  What caused _____ to happen?
- Observe the person's body language when he or she responds.
- Pay attention to the person's tone of voice.
- Listen to the spoken language used in the response.
  o Which words does the person use? Are they neutral, descriptive, or explanatory?

Record your experience on the log on the next page.

Why/How, What Exercise Log: Body Language, Tone of Voice, Language Used

	Why	How, What
Describe Body Language	_____	_____
	_____	_____
Describe the Tone of Voice	_____	_____
	_____	_____
Name Some of the Words	_____	_____
	_____	_____

Chapter 4: Swing Words and Phrases

eople often use words and phrases they consider positive, when in fact, the words and phrases they have chosen are negative. The difference is not evident until you replace the word or phrase with Action Based Communication's swing words and phrases. Shifts experienced with swing words and phrases are slightly less forceful than those experienced with power words.

> "Understanding how language shapes a situation gives you greater control of the situation. It provides a workbox of useful tools and a way to think about language choices that can change minds and increase options." (McGinty, p. 7)

Let's experience how the quote relates to the swing words and phrases.

Summary of Swing Word and Phrase Choices	
Disruption	Connection
Get Over, Around	Get Through
Hanging In	Staying With
Hope	Trust, Expect
Need	Want
Not Bad	Pretty Good
Think, Feel, Believe, Know	Omit think, feel, believe, know

Get Over, Around/Through

One of the most commonly used swing phrases is *get over* it. Almost as common is the phrase *get around* it. People use *get over* or *get around* interchangeably, making others feel better—or at least they think that they are providing support or help.

Look at the difference in the effects of these swing phrases by visualizing the action and the energy spent to *get over*, *get around*, and *get through* a brick wall, illustrated in Figures 6, 7, and 8. Apply the principle of energy conservation as you look at each figure.

Over

A colleague tells you to ***get over*** something. How do you feel?

When people are angry, disappointed, or have experienced a loss or failure, or encountered the unexpected they need to use their energy for reflection or grieving. Reflection creates space so people can use their energy to gain clarity. Grieving creates space so people can use their energy to heal.

Examples

- You will ***get over*** losing your job.
- You will ***get over*** making the mistake.
- You will ***get over*** the disagreement with your team members.

Figure 6: Get Over It

Getting ***over*** a hurdle requires using extra energy; so does getting over an emotional reaction. As illustrated in Figure 6, the anger, issue, obstacle, disappointment, loss, failure, or unexpected remains unchanged.

Telling someone who is angry or has experienced disappointment, loss, or failure to *get over* it encourages that person to stay angry. *Get over* also discourages healing and can immobilize the person from taking positive action. *Get over* impedes progress and disrupts the opportunity for reflection and the natural healing cycle. *Get over* also increases stress and tension and negates the person's feelings.

Around

Your friend tells you about a difficult experience with a co-worker. Your friend needs to use her energy to understand and manage the situation so she can deal with the difficulty.

Advising your friend to *get around* it actually creates more obstacles and increases difficulty. Your advice to *get around* it encourages her to avoid managing the difficulty. As advice, *get around* also may increase stress and tension.

Examples

- You will *get around* losing your job.
- You will *get around* making the mistake.
- You will *get around* the disagreement with your team members.

As you can see in Figure 7, a person who **gets around** an issue or works **around** a difficulty or moves **around** the unexpected travels on an indirect path. The obstacle, difficulty, or unexpected (brick wall) remains unchanged.

Figure 7: Get Around It

Get around also impedes progress and disrupts the direct approach to managing difficulties, again using extra energy to get nowhere.

Through

If you were angry or experienced disappointment, loss, failure, or the unexpected what would it be like for you to hear, "You will **get through** it?"

What would it be like for you if you had a difficult experience to hear, "You will *get through* it?"

Examples

- You will *get through* losing your job.
- You will *get through* making the mistake.
- You will *get through* the disagreement with your team members.

Offering encouragement and an indication that you will *get through* something is empathizing and helps conserve energy needed to deal with the difficulty, work through the disappointment, loss, or failure, or face the unexpected.

In Figure 8, the person who was told *get through* it travels a straight path. The obstacle, difficulty, loss, failure, or unexpected (brick wall) is no longer intact.

Figure 8: Get Through It

When offered the comfort of *get through* it, people usually see and experience events differently. The obstacle, disappointment, difficulty, loss, or unexpected (brick wall) actually changes. Because the shape of the issue has changed, you see and experience it differently.

Get through creates a connection and keeps the natural cycle of progress moving forward.

Choose the swing phrase *get through*
Experience the Joy of Connection

Work Less to Get More with Get Through: Activity I

The purpose of this exercise is to help you become aware of your experience hearing *get over*. You will need to work with a partner.

- Ask your partner to say, "You will ***get over*** your mistake."
- Repeat

Record the experience of what happened in your body and your feelings.

Get Over

Physical
Experience

_____

_____

_____

Feelings

_____

_____

_____

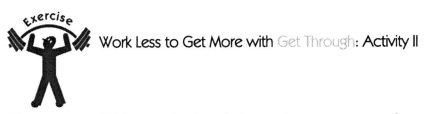

The purpose of this exercise is to help you become aware of your experience hearing **_get around_**. You will need to work with a partner.

- Ask your partner to say, "You will **_get around_** your mistake."
- Repeat

Record the experience of what happened in your body and your feelings.

Get Around

Physical
Experience
_____

_____

_____

Feelings
_____

_____

_____

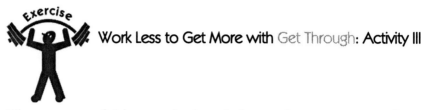

The purpose of this exercise is to help you become aware of your experience hearing *get through*. You will need to work with a partner.

- Ask your partner to say, "You will *get through* your mistake."
- Repeat

Record the experience of what happened in your body and your feelings.

Get Through

Physical
Experience

_____

_____

_____

Feelings

_____

_____

_____

Hanging In/Staying With

One of the easiest phrases of Action Based Communication's swing words to visualize is *hanging in*.

Hanging in

Hanging in is frequently used to communicate what people believe is positive. Some variation of "I'm hanging in there" is often given as the response to the question, "How's it going?" *Hanging in* is also frequently the response others offer upon hearing something that might not be going well.

Visualize *hanging in*. What are you hanging from? What are you hanging onto? Visualize *hanging* on to a tree branch.

Check your comfort level. How do you feel? How would you rate your level of security?

Hanging in is a vulnerable position. The phrase implies being close to letting go altogether and falling. A person who is *hanging in* could easily fall or slip. A strong wind might cause the person to lose his or her grip. Now that's disruption!

Even if your grip were secure, *hanging in* leaves you ungrounded. Creating a connection from such a position is highly unlikely.

Note your reaction to the following exchanges:
- How are you doing with the new project?

  I'm *hanging in* there
- How are you?

  I'm *hanging in* there
- How is your team managing with the new equipment?

  We're *hanging in* there

Staying with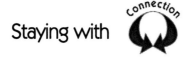

How might you feel if instead of *hanging in* you told someone you were *staying with* it? What would you hear and how would you experience support for a difficult experience you were having with *staying with* it?

Staying with communicates strength and stability. Visualize *staying with* or an alternative phrase, *standing your ground*.

The latter provides a sense of being grounded.

Pay attention to how you feel when *staying with* or some variant of *standing your ground* replaces *hanging in*:
- How are you doing with the new project?

  I'm *staying with* it

- How are you?
  I'm *standing my ground*
- How is your team managing with the new equipment?
  We're *staying with* it

Practicing with the exercise will deepen your experience of saying and hearing *hanging in* and *staying with*.

Use examples from your life to explore the shift in your experience and feelings using the swing phrases *hanging in* and *staying with*.

Choose the swing phrase *staying with*
Experience the Joy of Connection

Exercise

Feel the Earth beneath Your Feet with Staying With: Activity I

The purpose of this exercise is to help you become aware of your experience saying *hanging in* and *staying with*.

- Respond out loud to the question, "How are things going?" First say, "I'm *hanging in*." Then respond saying, "I'm *staying with* the program."
- Vary your tone of voice

Record the experience of what happened in your body and your feelings. Note shifts when substituting *staying with* for *hanging in*.

	Hanging In	Staying With
Physical Experience	_____	_____
	_____	_____
	_____	_____
Feelings	_____	_____
	_____	_____
	_____	_____

Feel the Earth beneath Your Feet with Staying With: Activity II

The purpose of this exercise is to help you become aware of your experience hearing *hanging in* and *staying with*.

- Ask a partner to respond to the question, "How are things going? Ask your partner to first respond with, "*Hanging in*" and then with "*Staying with*."
- Request the partner to vary his or her tone of voice.

Record the experience of what happened in your body and your feelings. Note shifts when substituting *staying with* for *hanging in*.

	Hanging In	Staying With
Physical Experience	_____	_____
	_____	_____
	_____	_____
Feelings	_____	_____
	_____	_____
	_____	_____

Hope/Trust, Expect

The relationship among the swing words *hope*, *trust*, and *expect* varies according to the environmental context in which the words are used.

Can you imagine the United States making progress if the motto on U.S. currency stated "In God We Hope?"

Let's examine how the swing words *hope*, *trust*, and *expect* apply in both business and personal settings.

Hope

Offering *hope* in a business context extends a sense of uncertainty and perhaps insecurity. *Hope* does not support desired outcomes. *Hope* communicates doubt. Some people experience *hope* as weak.

Example

In a conversation I had with a client about an upcoming job interview, she offered, "I *hope* things will turn out OK." I asked her to tell me how she experienced herself saying *hope*, and she responded, "Weak."

If you *hope* to sell a product or be selected for a position, chances are good you will spend too much time on and be less effective in landing either the sale or the position. *Hope* disrupts the process of securing a sale or a position.

Remember a time when you got an outcome easily rather than with difficulty. Were you *hoping*, *trusting*, or *expecting* that you would succeed?

Trust

Replacing *hope* with *trust* or *expect* communicates certainty; *trust* and *expect* convey strength. *Hope* does not offer a sense of security; *trust* and *expect* do.

Offering *trust* or *expect* extends support for reaching desired outcomes. *Trust* and *expect* create a connection.

Trust and *expect* pull to completion.

Jennifer

Immediately before the first presentation of a workshop she developed, Jennifer received an e-mail from her colleague Chip, saying, "I *trust* your session this afternoon will go well."

As she read the e-mail, Jennifer sat up straighter, pushing her shoulders back and putting both feet on the floor. She smiled and felt excited about delivering the workshop. Chip's message bolstered her confidence.

How might she have felt had Chip written, "I *hope* your presentation will go well?" How would you feel?
Visualize your posture. How would you be sitting?

Get a sense of your experience as you read the following examples.

Examples

- I *hope* this work I'm doing to secure a new position will lead to a job I love.
- I *trust* this work I'm doing to secure a new position will lead to a job I love.
- I *expect* this work I'm doing to secure a new position will lead to a job I love.

- I *hope* the deal goes through.
- I *trust* the deal will go through.
- I *expect* the deal will go through.

- We *hope* the services were to your satisfaction.
- We *trust* the services were to your satisfaction.
- We *expect* the services were to your satisfaction.

In a business context use *trust* or *expect* to create a connection or reach a goal. *Trust* and *expect* communicate strength and certainty.

 Listen to the speaker's tone of voice when you hear someone say *hope* or *trust* or *expect*. With hope the voice usually sounds weak or faint; with *trust* and *expect*, strong or full.

As the adage about winners and losers says, "What's the difference between winners and losers? Winners *expect* to win, losers only *hope* to." Be a winner. Use *trust* or *expect*.

Now let's explore the swing when shifting from business matters to personal ones with some examples that illustrate the difference.

Examples

- I *hope* I will win the lottery.
- I *trust* I will win the lottery.
- I *expect* I will win the lottery.

- I *hope* the guests had a good time.
- I *trust* the guests had a good time.
- I *expect* the guests had a good time.

- I *hope* things work out with moving to a new city.
- I *trust* things to work out with moving to a new city.
- I *expect* things to work out with moving to a new city.

On the personal side, sometimes *hope* is all people have with which to sustain themselves. In personal matters, *hope* may be the only thing people use for support. Compared to the business context, in the personal context, *hope* communicates optimism and strength. As Daniel Goleman explains:

> From the perspective of emotional intelligence, having *hope* means that one will not give in to overwhelming anxiety, a defeatist attitude, or depression in the face of difficult challenges or setbacks. Optimism, like *hope*, means having a strong *expectation* that in general, things will turn out all right in life . . . . (Goleman, pp. 87-88; bold and italics are mine)

Choose the swing words *trust* and *expect* for business matters
Choose the swing word *hope* for personal matters
Experience the Joy of Connection

 Work Out Business Matters with Trust or Expect: Activity I

The purpose of this exercise is to help you become aware of your experience saying *hope* and **trust** or **expect** related to business matters.

- Say first, "I *hope* the deal will go through." Then say, "I **trust** or **expect** the deal will go through."
- Vary your tone of voice

Record the experience of what happened in your body and your feelings. Note shifts when substituting **trust** or **expect** for **hope**.

	Hope	Trust or Expect
Physical Experience	_____	_____
	_____	_____
	_____	_____
Feelings	_____	_____
	_____	_____
	_____	_____

Exercise

Work Out Business Matters with Trust or Expect: Activity II

The purpose of this exercise is to help you become aware of your experience hearing *hope* and *trust* or *expect* related to business matters.

- Ask a partner to say first, "I *hope* the deal will go through." Then ask your partner to say, "I *trust* or *expect* the deal will go through."
- Request the partner to vary his or her tone of voice.

Record the experience of what happened in your body and your feelings. Note shifts substituting *trust* or *expect* for *hope*.

	Hope	Trust or Expect
Physical Experience	_____	_____
	_____	_____
	_____	_____
Feelings	_____	_____
	_____	_____
	_____	_____

Work Out Personal Matters with Hope: Activity I

The purpose of this exercise is to help you become aware of your experience saying *trust* or *expect* and *hope* related to personal matters.

- Say first, "I *expect* or *trust* I will win the lottery." Then say, "I *hope* I will win the lottery."
- Vary your tone of voice

Record the experience of what happened in your body and your feelings. Note shifts when substituting *hope* for *trust* or *expect*.

	Trust or Expect	Hope
Physical Experience	_____	_____
	_____	_____
	_____	_____
Feelings	_____	_____
	_____	_____
	_____	_____

The purpose of this exercise is to help you become aware of your experience hearing *trust* or *expect* and *hope* related to personal matters.

- Ask a partner to say first, "I *trust* or *expect* I will win the lottery." Then ask your partner to say, "I *hope* I will win the lottery."
- Request the partner to vary his or her tone of voice.

Record the experience of what happened in your body and your feelings. Note shifts with the substitution of *hope* for *trust* or *expect*.

	Trust or Expect	Hope
Physical Experience	_____	_____
	_____	_____
	_____	_____
Feelings	_____	_____
	_____	_____
	_____	_____

Need/Want

The swing between *need* (requirement or deprivation) and *want* (preference or desire) is similar to the swing between *hope* and *trust* or *expect*. Exchanging *need* for *want* and *want* for *need* gains strength according to the environmental context in which the word is used.

Need

The sales person who approaches creating a connection—making a sale—from the basis of *need* (requirement or deprivation) spends unnecessary time and energy securing that sale. The underlying sense of deprivation quietly communicates to the customer and disrupts the sales person's sense of self worth, let alone his or her sales quota.

In personal terms, people refer to their *need* for a significant other, some to the point of inability to function effectively without one.

Needing another person to complete your existence focuses attention on the requirement or deprivation, the lack of a partner. This often makes it difficult to be fully available to create a connection with a potential significant other.

In sales and personal settings, *need* depletes energy and pushes away. *Want* energizes and pulls toward.

Want

The sales person who approaches creating a connection— making a sale—from the basis of *want* (preference or desire) creates a different experience. That person makes efficient use of his or her energy in securing a sale. The underlying sense of desire maintains the sales person's engagement in closing the deal.

On the personal side, the *want* (preference or desire) for a partner fills one with a sense of excitement about the process of creating a connection with a significant other.

Now let's explore the swing when using *need* and *want* in management situations.

Want

When a superior says, "I *want* you to undertake a project," how certain are you of the requirement? Do you have a sense of when the work is due?

While *want* in this case may not be a clear disruption, *want* does not create a connection in the way that *need* does.

Need

When a superior says, "I **need** you to undertake a project," do you hear and fully understand the urgency of getting the work done? Would you get the same sense of urgency if a superior said, "I **want** you to undertake a project?" Compare the following request:

- "We **need** the report in the next few days."
- "We **want** the report in the next few days."

To which request would you respond more quickly?

In management, requests made in terms of **need** create a connection. Action is more likely to occur when requests are stated in the active sense, as "I **need**" or "you **need**."

In this context, **need** energizes and pulls toward, and carries an almost survival imperative. **Need** attracts energy and supports connection. **Want** evokes instinctive resistance.

Choose the swing word *want* for sales and personal matters
Choose the swing word *need* for management situations
Experience the Joy of Connection

Get What You Want in Sales or Other Business Matters

The purpose of this exercise is to help you become aware of your experience saying *need* and *want* related to sales or business.

- Say first, "I *need* to exceed my sales quota." Then say, "I *want* to exceed my sales quota."

Record the experience of what happened in your body and your feelings. Note shifts when substituting *want* for *need*.

	Need	Want
Physical Experience	_____	_____
	_____	_____
	_____	_____
Feelings	_____	_____
	_____	_____
	_____	_____

The purpose of this exercise is to help you become aware of your experience saying *need* and *want* related to personal matters.

- Say first, "I *need* a life partner to have a good existence." Then say, "I *want* a life partner to have a good existence."

Record the experience of what happened in your body and your feelings. Note shifts when substituting *want* for *need*.

	Need	Want
Physical Experience	_____	_____
	_____	_____
	_____	_____
Feelings	_____	_____
	_____	_____
	_____	_____

The purpose of this exercise is to help you become aware of your experience saying *need* and *want* as a manager.

- Imagine talking with a direct report.
- Say out loud first, "I *want* the report completed." Then say, "I *need* the report completed."

Record the experience of what happened in your body and your feelings. Note shifts when substituting *need* for *want*.

	Want	Need
Physical Experience	_____	_____
	_____	_____
	_____	_____
Feelings	_____	_____
	_____	_____
	_____	_____

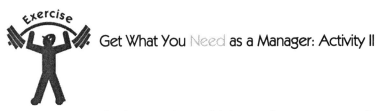

Get What You Need as a Manager: Activity II

The purpose of this exercise, which requires a partner, is to help you become aware of your experience hearing *want* and *need* as a direct report.

- Ask your partner to say first, "I *want* the report completed" and then to say, "I *need* the report completed."

Record the experience of what happened in your body and your feelings. Note shifts when *need* replaced *want*.

	Need	Want
Physical Experience	_____ _____	_____ _____
Feelings	_____ _____ _____	_____ _____ _____

Not Bad/Pretty Good

Which would you rather hear about the quality of your work—*not bad* or *pretty good?*

Not bad

Not bad is used so frequently to communicate what people believe is positive that you may not realize how negative you sound. Replacing *not bad* with a positive phrase that communicates the same idea changes how you sound and your experience.

What do you hear when someone says *not bad* about their general state of well being? How do feel when comments about your work are *not bad?* *Not bad* is an expression of the absence of something. *Not bad* is a reprieve.

Not and *bad* are both negative words. Putting the words together is a double whammy.

Note your reaction to the following exchanges:

- How does it look for the meeting next week?
  Not bad
- How is the new project going?
  Not bad

- How do I look?

  Not bad

- How do you feel?

  Not bad

Pretty good

If you are asked a question to which you would normally respond *not bad*, experiment by responding with *pretty good*.

Pay attention to how you feel when *pretty good* replaces *not bad* in the same exchanges as above.

- How does it look for the meeting next week?

  Pretty good

- How is the new project going?

  Pretty good

- How do I look?

  Pretty good

- How do you feel?

  Pretty good

Pretty and *good* are both positive words. Putting the words together is a double bonus.

If you are face to face with the receiver, watch his or her face to get a sense of how he or she feels upon hearing *pretty good*.

> ... when a person's words disagree with what is conveyed via his tone of voice, gesture, ... the emotional truth is in **how** he says something rather than in **what** he says.
>
> Daniel Goleman

For this swing phrase, if you are the receiver of *not bad*, pay attention to the speaker's tone of voice, which can provide clues about her or his feelings.

Goleman's message in the sidebar underscores the importance of paying attention to tone of voice. Doing so helps to understand the emotional content you are delivering.

Gloria and Gene

Gloria and Gene shared office space as independent CPAs, each with separate clients. Gloria arrived before Gene and left after him most days. Each day upon Gene's arrival, Gloria asked him how he was, and he responded, "*not bad.*" At the end of the day when Gene was leaving, Gloria asked him how his day had been, and he responded, "*not bad.*"

After awhile Gloria started feeling less than her usual upbeat self when she was in the office. She could not figure out what was causing the slight shift. She checked the space for any environmental changes that might have contributed to her mood swing. Finding nothing, she began to assess her relationship with Gene. That examination yielded nothing to explain the shift.

Finally Gloria mentioned her concern to a friend and shared the conversation that began and ended each day. Gloria's friend listened and offered to play the role of Gene. In doing so, she responded to "How are you?" and "How was your day?" with "*pretty good*"rather than "*not bad*." Gloria was able to substitute *pretty good* silently each time Gene responded *not bad*. The reframing made a difference; Gloria began feeling better. Later she told Gene about the substitution she was making, and encouraged him to make the same one.

Choose the swing phrase *pretty good*
Experience the Joy of Connection

Lift Up with Pretty Good: Activity I

The purpose of this exercise is to help you become aware of your experience saying ***not bad*** and ***pretty good***.

- Say first, "My performance at work is ***not bad***." Then say, "My performance at work is ***pretty good***."
- Vary your tone of voice

Record the experience of what happened in your body and your feelings. Note shifts when substituting ***pretty good*** for ***not bad***.

	Not Bad	Pretty Good
Physical Experience	_____	_____
	_____	_____
	_____	_____
Feelings	_____	_____
	_____	_____
	_____	_____

Lift Up with Pretty Good: **Activity II**

The purpose of this exercise is to help you become aware of your experience hearing *not bad* and *pretty good*.

- Ask a partner to say first, "Your performance at work is *not bad*." Then ask your partner to say, "Your performance at work is *pretty good*."
- Request the partner to vary his or her tone of voice.

Record the experience of what happened in your body and your feelings. Note shifts with the substitution of *pretty good* for *not bad*.

	Not Bad	Pretty Good
Physical Experience	_____	_____
	_____	_____
	_____	_____
Feelings	_____	_____
	_____	_____
	_____	_____

nk, Feel, Believe, Know/
ne of the choices

Included in swing words and phrases is a progression commonly used in sales training: moving from *think* to *feel* to *believe* to *know* to eliminating *think*, *feel*, *believe*, and *know*.

Figure 9: Think, Feel, Believe, Know Progression

Think, Feel, Believe, Know

In sales presentations, *think*, *feel*, *believe*, and *know* clutter the space between you and your desired outcome. The words are fillers that disrupt the communication flow. Creating a connection requires open space.

Athletic coaches encourage the performer to "act as if" she or he has won. Directors also use the same routine of "acting as if" with stage performers. Business coaches use this method as well to help sales people improve presentations. Working with clients along the *think*, *feel*, *believe*, *know* progression helps them "act as if" they have won, in this case, the particular sale.

Imagine you are the marketing manager for a consumer products company and are considering buying a customer relationship management system. To help make the decision, you requested oral proposals from five different vendors. Marketing representatives from five companies made product presentations to you.

- The person from Company A stated, "I *think* our customer relationship management system exceeds your requirements."
- The person from Company B stated, "I *feel* our customer relationship management system exceeds your requirements."
- The person from Company C stated, "I *believe* our customer relationship management system exceeds your requirements."
- The person from Company D stated, "I *know* our customer relationship management exceeds system your requirements."
- The person from Company E stated, "Our consulting customer relationship management system exceeds your requirements."

Which company appeals to you the most? Which company created a connection?

In sales presentations coaching, I observe clients' body language and hear their voices change as they move along the *think*, *feel*, *believe*, *know* progression. The progression moves along a path toward increasing certainty.

Clients reported feeling uncertain when they first rehearsed using their own words, which commonly were *think*, *feel*, *believe*. Their voices and bodies reflected that uncertainty. When they rehearsed with, "I *know*/we *know* our method . . . ." they reported a sense that they were beginning to create a connection with the potential buyer of their services. Their voices were stronger and they stood up straighter when they said *know*.

An even stronger connection is possible if none of the above words is used: "Our method. . . ." Eliminating *think*, *feel*, *believe*, and *know* creates a simple, clear, direct route to a connection.

Examples

- I *think* our product is the best in its class.
- I *feel* our product is the best in its class.
- I *believe* our product is the best in its class.
- I *know* our product is the best in its class.
- Our product is the best in its class.

In communication there is a saying, "When in doubt, leave it out." Here, "Prevent doubt, leave it out." Particularly in sales, with the *think*, *feel*, *believe*, *know* progression, the strongest message is conveyed when *think*, *feel*, *believe*, or *know* is eliminated.

Omit *think, feel, believe, know*
Experience the Joy of Connection

Practice the Think, Feel, Believe, Know **Workout:**
Activity I—Think

In this series of exercises, practice eliminating from your language *think*, *feel*, *believe*, and *know*. Record the experience of what happened in your body and your feelings as you move through each word in the progression.

Say out loud the sentence, "I _**think**_ our system provides the most efficient and effective results."

Think

Physical
Experience
_____

_____

_____

Feelings
_____

_____

_____

Practice the Think, Feel, Believe, Know **Workout:**
Activity II—Feel

Record the experience of what happened in your body and your feelings when you say out loud, "I _**feel**_ our system provides the most efficient and effective results."

Feel

Physical
Experience

_____

_____

_____

Feelings

_____

_____

_____

Practice the Think, Feel, Believe, Know **Workout:**
Activity III—Believe

Record the experience of what happened in your body and your feelings when you say out loud, "I _**believe**_ our system provides the most efficient and effective results."

Believe

Physical
Experience
_____

_____

_____

Feelings
_____

_____

_____

Practice the Think, Feel, Believe, Know **Workout:**
Activity IV—Know

Record the experience of what happened in your body and your feelings when you say out loud, "I _**know**_ our system provides the most efficient and effective results."

Know

Physical
Experience
_____

_____

_____

Feelings
_____

_____

_____

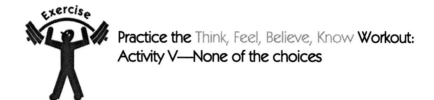

Practice the Think, Feel, Believe, Know **Workout:**
Activity V—None of the choices

Record the experience of what happened in your body and your feelings when you say, "Our system provides the most efficient and effective results."

Omitted think, feel, believe, and know

Physical
Experience

_____

_____

_____

Feelings

_____

_____

_____

Chapter 5: Throwaway Words

his chapter recommends discarding certain throwaway words. People often use these words to deal with something uncomfortable, hiding behind them to mask true meaning and avoid being direct.

You can change experience and create connections by eliminating the throwaway words.

Summary of Throwaway Words	
Disruption	Connection
Interesting	*Omit*
Nice	*Omit*
Should, Could, Would, Must	*Omit*
Try	*Omit*

Interesting

What do you mean when you say *interesting*?

Interesting . . .
hmm
Hmm . . .
interesting

What do you understand others to mean whey they say *interesting*?

How often do you use *interesting* when you do not want to say something negative?

Interesting really says nothing.
Interesting—

- Often covers up meaning
- Is an example of fuzzy thinking
- Can be used to be strategically ambiguous
- Is a euphemism
- Can be used as a placeholder to give the speaker a second or two to construct a better response

In a beta test of Action Based Communication, workshop participants indicated they often used interesting to avoid saying something negative. I learned that many told their colleagues that training programs they were required to attend were interesting when they actually thought they were boring. Participants also said that in describing an action to people they did not know or did not know well, they would use *interesting*. If they were describing the same action to a friend, they would say, "Dumb."

On November 30, 2004, a Fox News cable network anchor initially commented on courtroom testimony at Scott Peterson's trial for the murder of his wife Laci and unborn son Conner as *interesting*. She stopped immediately upon saying it to offer that interesting was not the best word to describe the event.

While I do not know the reason for her comment, the anchor may have realized she was hiding behind *interesting*, because in previous broadcasts about the same trial she had made more direct statements.

Example

In showing a friend a ring I designed she said, "Oh, that's *interesting*." I knew instantly that she did not like it.

I said, "You don't like it, do you? Saying *interesting* often covers up something negative. "

She said, "No, and I didn't want to tell you that. It's not my taste."

She was being a good friend and probably thought she was avoiding hurting my feelings by using the word *interesting*.

Curious, different, fascinating, and intriguing are possible alternatives for *interesting*. The best alternative is to remain silent. As someone once said, "If you don't have anything nice to say, don't say anything at all."

Throw away *interesting*
Experience the Joy of Connection

Nice

How many times have you heard, "Isn't that *nice*," to describe someone's action, appearance, or an experience? Do you comment after attending an event that you had a *nice* time when you really did not?

What about after being introduced, as in *nice* to meet you? Do you describe the person as *nice* because you do not know what else to say? Would you want to be described as *nice*?

Nice is the poor relative of *interesting* and is another word that people sometimes use to avoid saying something negative. At best, *nice* is lukewarm praise. Nonetheless, *nice* may be interpreted as negative—or as a positive that is so weak that it is negative by default and association.

If you hear someone say *interesting* or *nice*, use the speaker's tone of voice and facial expression to help you decide if either word is a subtle negative. If talking on the phone, rely on the person's tone of voice.

When you want to avoid saying something that could be interpreted as negative, consider using enjoyable and pleasant for events and decent for people as possible alternatives for *nice*.

The Language Reframing Log, Chapter 7, includes *interesting* and *nice* so you can compare your experience using each word with your experience omitting each word.

Throw away *nice*
Experience the Joy of Connection

Should, Could, Would, Must

The words *should*, *could*, *would*, and *must* cause a disruption and set the stage for disappointment or another negative response or reaction. *Should*, *could*, and *would* are coercive; *must* is imperative.

- *Should*—Sets up an opportunity for making a value judgment and for avoiding responsibility. *Should* is a public announcement of intention not to do something and conditions the intention not to occur.

  If you say you *should* do something and you don't do it, you probably feel bad.

- *Could*—Sets up an opportunity for avoidance.

  If you say you *could* do something and don't do it, you may feel guilty.

- *Would*—Sets up an opportunity for disappointment.

  If you say you *would* do something and don't do it, you may feel as if you let yourself or someone else down.

- *Must*—Guarantees making a value judgment and taps into issues of moral obligation.

  If you say you *must* do something and don't do it, you may feel both bad and guilty.

Examples

I *should* exercise every day, and if I do not, I feel as though I failed.

Those who do not love to exercise might never do it if exercising is stated as a *should*. I am *willing* to exercise every day creates a more likely possibility for exercise to occur.

I *must* save 25 percent of my gross earnings. I may judge myself as inadequate if I do not save that percent.

I am more likely to fail at saving than if I said instead, "I *want* to save 25 percent of my gross earnings." The latter creates enthusiasm and energy for achieving the desired goal.

Should, *could*, *would*, and *must* push away. *Must* is the next of kin of *should*. Both words are coercive and invite resistance. They cause a disruption if you are the speaker or hearer.

You create space for connections when you throw away *should* and *must*.

Instead of *should*, use *willing*. Replace *must* with *want*.

By changing a single word or reframing, you offer yourself and others a new way of looking at situations and a new way of experiencing them.

Should, *could*, *would*, and *must* live on a cul de sac named "Can't." The words are dead ends that leave no room for creating connections.

Figure 10: The Can't Cul de Sac

How do you feel when you tell yourself or hear *should*, *could*, *would*, and *must*? Are you aware of any shift in your physical structure?

Throw away should, could, would, must
Experience the Joy of Connection

Exercise

What Course Are You Charting With Should?

The purpose of this series of exercises is to help you become aware of physical sensation and feelings saying **should**, **could**, **would**, and **must**.

Record the experience of what happened in your body and your feelings when you say out loud, "I _**should**_ drink eight glasses of water every day."

Should

Physical
Experience

_____

_____

_____

Feelings

_____

_____

_____

What Course Are You Charting With Could?

Record the experience of what happened in your body and your feelings when you say out loud, "I _**could**_ drink eight glasses of water every day."

Could

Physical
Experience

_____

_____

_____

Feelings

_____

_____

_____

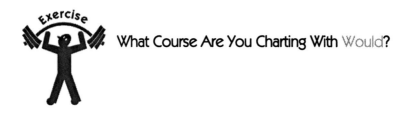

What Course Are You Charting With Would?

Record the experience of what happened in your body and your feelings when you say out loud, "I ___*would*___ drink eight glasses of water every day."

Would

**Physical
Experience**

_____

_____

_____

Feelings

_____

_____

_____

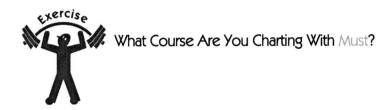

Exercise

What Course Are You Charting With Must?

Record the experience of what happened in your body and your feelings when you say out loud, "I **_must_** drink eight glasses of water every day."

	Must
Physical Experience	
Feelings	

Try

Have you ever *tried* something new? Have you ever *tried* to change your behavior?

In reality, none of us has ever *tried* anything (unless you are an attorney who has tried cases in court). We either do something, or we do not.

Visualize *try*.
What does *try* look like?

Touch *try*.
What does *try* feel like?

Can you describe what you do when you *try*?
What results can you show when you *try*?

Is this "trying" your patience?

You probably had a difficult time visualizing *try*, explaining what *try* feels like, and describing what you do when you *try*. This is precisely the issue with using *try*. The end result of *try* is, in fact, nothing.

Try is the declaration of effort with implicit failure.

Some people in organizational communication believe that *try* allows for failure in a respectful way.

Try does nothing to support creating connections. In testing Action Based Communication, some people said they use *try* when they did not want to work, think, or expend any energy. Other people said they use *try* to hide from the fact that they did nothing. *Try* is the same as not.

$$Try = 0$$

Try is similar to *but* and is used unconsciously and frequently. Instead of *try*, use any of the following alternatives:

- Attempt
- Experiment
- Explore
- Play
- Practice
- Sample
- Test
- Work

Or as my British friends say, "Give it a go."

Examples

- *Attempt* to sing in the shower
- *Experiment* with singing in the shower
- *Explore* singing in the shower
- *Play* with singing in the shower
- *Practice* singing in the shower
- *Sample* singing in the shower
- *Test* singing in the shower
- *Work* at singing in the shower

In each of the examples some activity occurred. Something happened.

Trying to Try **is Trying: Measuring** Try

A chair or bottle or glass of water is required to do this exercise.

- Sit in the chair
- Take a few seconds to *try* getting out of the chair

Or

- Place the bottle or glass of water at arm's length
- Take a few seconds to *try* picking up the glass or bottle
- Note each specific action you took to *try* getting out of the chair or to *try* picking up the bottle or glass of water in the spaces below.

Action 1 _____

Action 2 _____

Action 3 _____

Action 4 _____

Action 5 _____

If you *try* to get out of the chair, you will find yourself still sitting in the chair. Either you get out of the chair or you do not. If you *try* to pick up the bottle or glass of water, you will notice that the soda can remains in its original location.

When you *try* to take action, you are doing absolutely nothing. With *try*, progress is not possible. With *try* creating a connection is not possible.

If you entered anything in the action spaces, your position changed (e.g., leaned forward, bent knees, moved arm). You didn't *try*, rather you expended energy, you moved, you worked, you acted. Once you complete an action, you no longer *try* it.

Throw away *try*
Experience the Joy of Connection

Chapter 6: The Apart/ A Part Model

n moving from internal dialogue to external dialogue, the focus is on using the body rather than the meaning of words to experience the difference between causing a disruption and creating a connection. The Apart/A Part Model is particularly useful in a range of circumstances including the following:

- Business transition—Merger, restructuring, promotion, new business owner, working for a new manager, inheriting a new team
- Charged situation—Frustrated or angry
- Stuck—Unable to let go or move on

The essential component of the Apart/A Part Model is space. You can see this from looking at the words themselves:

- Apart

- A Part

Space is a requirement for creating connections. Without space there is no room to connect. There are various forms of space.

- Aural—Quiet makes it easier for some people to make connections in their thinking process. Active listening is needed to create a positive connection with another person. Space is an integral part of active listening. Musical scores contain space between notes or measures that allows the listener to connect the two and hear a theme. Space in the form of time between words in spoken language allows the listener to connect the words.

- Optical—White space or unprinted space (margins, space between lines and paragraphs) you see in books makes it easier for the reader to connect with the material.

- Physical—*External*: Area between you and other people or you and physical objects. Moving away from people or physical objects (e.g., computer that suddenly developed a personality disorder) makes creating a connection or reconnection easier. *Internal*: Space between vertebrae is needed to be able move in a connected way. Space is needed between teeth to prevent decay.

- Temporal—Time separates events, which allows the mind to get clear and ready to create a connection.

Let's explore the Apart/A Part Model by looking at two sets of circles. Each set represents a different or opposite way you might work through a transition, frustration, or anger, or get unstuck from almost anything you do not like, or with which you are uncomfortable, or from your thought patterns.

Set A—Stuck/Limited Options

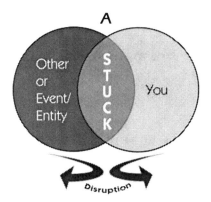

In using the models, think of "You" as representing yourself, "Other" as representing another person, and any of the following as an "Event/Entity:"

- Change in job status
- New management team
- Technology failure

In Set A the circles overlap, restricting action, movement, or progress. Consider the area in which the circles overlap—the common area they share—as stuck.

Let's take a closer look.

In Set A, "You" cannot move independently from "Other" or "Event/Entity" because there is no clear boundary separating the two circles. Everywhere "You" goes, "Other" or "Event/Entity" goes.

"You" and "Other" or "Event/Entity" occupy some of the same space. Sharing space makes operating independently impossible.

Example

You were let go from a company that was downsizing. During your search for a new position you kept thinking about being let go. Your job search was stuck with being let go (event); you were unable to search independently of the event.

When any two objects are *a part* of one another, as in Set A, there is no way to separate the objects from one another. This makes forward movement or positive connection impossible.

Set B—Freedom/Expanded Options

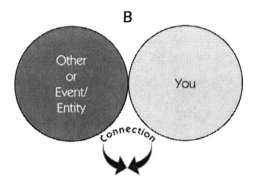

In Set B, the circles touch at only one point. The only common area is the single point of connection. "You" and "Other" or "Event/Entity" can move independently and freely.

For example, if "You" wanted to move from any one point on the circumference to any other single point on "Other's" or Event/Entity's" circumference, "You" could do so freely.

Set B offers the space that is required for creating connections. Because "You" and "Other" or "Event/Entity" only touch at one point without being bound to each other, they are free to be *apart*. This freedom makes creating a positive connection or joining, being *a part*, possible. "Other" or "Event/Entity" and "You" have the choice to be *a part*. In Set A, choosing to be *a part* is not possible.

People often get stuck when they go through a transition, and at times they are unable to work or talk themselves through being stuck. Here is where using the body first helps support creating a connection. Creating connections (being *a part* of a system) requires being separate (*apart*) and being able to detach (be *apart*) from whatever is keeping you stuck.

Gretchen and Francine

After 40+ years as a family owned and operated design firm, only two members remained: Francine, the widow of the firm's founder on the east coast; and her only child Gretchen, on the west coast. Francine decided to move to where Gretchen lived and operate the business only from there.

In the months before the move, Gretchen spent approximately 65 percent of her time on the east coast, assessing the physical and financial feasibility of what to move. Even though Francine made all the financial decisions, Gretchen was more active and engaged in the business and developed the moving plan.

During the final weeks before the move, Gretchen's frustration with her mother who "did not listen to anything I offered" matched her mother's growing sense of anxiety. Francine and Gretchen were unable to operate *apart* or independently from each other. Each was unable to understand the other's perspective.

Gretchen asked me what she could do to disengage or disentangle herself from her constant state of frustration and annoyance. I suggested doing "To Be A Part, Be Apart" Activity II (clearing space by swinging your arms) each time she felt her frustration rising.

A few days later, Gretchen reported that she felt less frustrated and better able to support her mother in moving and accepted her mother's inability to let go of some possessions. By moving *apart* or separating or creating distance, Gretchen was able to be *a part* and join.

In each of the three exercises that follow, you will use a different method to experience how being *apart* is required for being *a part* or joining or connecting. In each, you create space between "You" and the "Other" or "Event/Entity." You can do Activities I and II alone. You will need a partner to do Activity III. In Activity I you will observe how being *apart* creates the opportunity for being *a part*, for connections. In Activities II and III you will experience physically how being *apart* is required to create connections.

Choose *Being Apart* **to** *Be a Part*
Experience the Joy of Connection

To Be Apart Be A Part: Activity I

Supplies

- Four sheets of construction paper, preferably each a different color
- Glue, paste, or scotch tape

Preparation

- Cut out four equal circles
- Arrange circles in front of you and label two as "A" or "Stuck" and two as "B" or "Freedom"

Limited options

- Paste both "A" circles together so they overlap in the middle.
- Move the pasted pair and observe how the two circles always move together.

Expanded options

- Rotate the two "B" circles (free moving, not pasted) so that at each revolution one point of one circle touches one point of the other circle.

Record your observations and associated thoughts on the log on the next page.

Apart/A Part Exercise Log I: Observations and Associated Thoughts

	Limited Options	Expanded Options
Observations	_____	_____
	_____	_____
	_____	_____
Associated Thoughts	_____	_____
	_____	_____
	_____	_____

Exercise

To Be Apart Be A Part: Activity II

- Stand with feet hip width apart and your arms hanging loosely at your sides.
- Visualize the "Other" or "Event/Entity" as a difficult boss or employee, a difficult situation in your workplace, some current transition, or an unpleasant experience.
- Hold your arms in front of you with the top of the hands together, as illustrated.
  - Imagine that the person, situation, unpleasant experience, or transition is in between the tops of your hands throughout the exercise.
- Push your hands apart, moving your arms to the side
  - Increase speed and force as you repeatedly push your arms to each side
  - Continue swinging your arms for one minute
- Notice the sensation from moving arms apart and from increasing speed and force

NOTE

Pushing your hands forward also works. However, by pushing away from your body while swinging the arms you create a greater energy field.

Record the physical sensation you experienced, your associated thoughts, and your feelings on the log below.

Apart/A Part Exercise Log II: Physical Sensation, Associated Thoughts, Feelings

Physical
Sensation

_____

_____

_____

Associated
Thoughts

_____

_____

_____

Feelings

_____

_____

_____

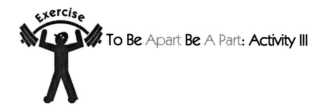

To Be Apart Be A Part: Activity III

Work with a partner, with both of you standing. Jointly select somewhere in the room (e.g., door in a room) and set this as your goal.

Limited options

- Walk with arms hooked at the elbow to the jointly selected goal
- Repeat

Can you and your partner arrive separately at the door? (This does not mean one person arriving early, because most assuredly, one person's foot will reach the goal—e.g., threshold if door is the goal—before the other person's foot.)

Expanded options

- Walk side-by-side with arms only touching at the elbow to the jointly selected goal
- Repeat

Describe the experience—what physically happened—and record your associated thoughts and feelings on the log on the next page.

Apart/A Part Exercise Log III: Experience, Associated Thoughts, Feelings

	Limited Options	Expanded Options
Describe Experience— What Physically Happened	_____ _____ _____	_____ _____ _____
Associated Thoughts	_____ _____ _____	_____ _____ _____
Feelings	_____ _____ _____	_____ _____ _____

Chapter 7: Language Reframing Log

The Language Reframing Log will enhance your learning process. The Log provides a place to record and measure your experiences using the choices in Power Words, Swing Words and Phrases, and Throwaway Words. Use the Log as you would a journal.

You can monitor and measure your progress over three phases:

- Getting Started—Current State or What Is
- Getting Settled—In Transition
- Moving Forward—Future State or New What Is

Each phase takes three weeks. We know from extensive studies about adult learning that three is the magic number or standard in changing experience or behavior.

Usually after three weeks of practice, people lose or let go of, or give up their previous behaviors. The behavior recedes from memory.

After another three weeks, people practice phasing in new behaviors. Practice is essential for retraining.

During the third, three-week period, people are integrating new behaviors.

Ideally, only 21 days are needed to develop a habit, with at most 90 days needed to push an old habit out of consciousness. For new habits to take fully may require 18 to 36 months. Once we learn a new practice or behavior, the learning stays with us. We do not really break old habits; we create new ones. The new habits push old habits down. The old habits take a back seat in the brain, as illustrated.

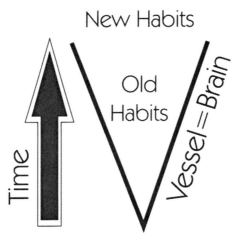

Figure 11: Shelf Life of Habits

The Log has three pages for each Power Word, Swing Word or Phrase, and Throwaway Word, one for each phase. Use the pages to measure how using or eliminating the words or phrases changes your experience over nine weeks. You will do exactly the same thing in each phase.

For each word in the Power Words and Swing Words and Phrases sections:

1. Record (using a hash mark or whatever you want to note your usage) each time you hear yourself use the word.

2. Circle the number on the scale that best represents your sense of either causing a disruption or creating a connection when you use the word, with 5 being a noticeable disruption and 1 being a clear connection.

For each word in the Throwaway Words section:

1. Describe your experience briefly.

   a. First use the word

   b. Then omit the word

2. For *try* there are also three pages to record your sense of causing a disruption or creating a connection when substituting any of the word choices for *try*.

Language Reframing Log
Messages You Send Your Brain
Power Words

Word	Frequency	Disruption				Connection
		Getting Started—Phase I				
But		5	4	3	2	1
		5	4	3	2	1
		5	4	3	2	1
		5	4	3	2	1
		5	4	3	2	1
		5	4	3	2	1
		5	4	3	2	1
		5	4	3	2	1
		5	4	3	2	1
		5	4	3	2	1
And		5	4	3	2	1
		5	4	3	2	1
		5	4	3	2	1
		5	4	3	2	1
		5	4	3	2	1
		5	4	3	2	1
		5	4	3	2	1
		5	4	3	2	1
		5	4	3	2	1
		5	4	3	2	1

Language Reframing Log
Power Words (cont)

Word	Frequency	Getting Settled—Phase II				
		Disruption				Connection
		5	4	3	2	1
		5	4	3	2	1
		5	4	3	2	1
		5	4	3	2	1
But		5	4	3	2	1
		5	4	3	2	1
		5	4	3	2	1
		5	4	3	2	1
		5	4	3	2	1
		5	4	3	2	1
		5	4	3	2	1
		5	4	3	2	1
		5	4	3	2	1
		5	4	3	2	1
And		5	4	3	2	1
		5	4	3	2	1
		5	4	3	2	1
		5	4	3	2	1
		5	4	3	2	1
		5	4	3	2	1

Language Reframing Log
Power Words (cont)

Word	Frequency	Moving Forward—Phase III				
		Disruption				Connection
		5	4	3	2	1
		5	4	3	2	1
		5	4	3	2	1
		5	4	3	2	1
But		5	4	3	2	1
		5	4	3	2	1
		5	4	3	2	1
		5	4	3	2	1
		5	4	3	2	1
		5	4	3	2	1
		5	4	3	2	1
		5	4	3	2	1
		5	4	3	2	1
		5	4	3	2	1
And		5	4	3	2	1
		5	4	3	2	1
		5	4	3	2	1
		5	4	3	2	1
		5	4	3	2	1
		5	4	3	2	1

Language Reframing Log
Power Words (cont)

Word	Frequency	Getting Started—Phase I				
		Disruption				Connection
		5	4	3	2	1
		5	4	3	2	1
		5	4	3	2	1
		5	4	3	2	1
Intend, Plan		5	4	3	2	1
		5	4	3	2	1
		5	4	3	2	1
		5	4	3	2	1
		5	4	3	2	1
		5	4	3	2	1
		5	4	3	2	1
		5	4	3	2	1
		5	4	3	2	1
		5	4	3	2	1
Will		5	4	3	2	1
		5	4	3	2	1
		5	4	3	2	1
		5	4	3	2	1
		5	4	3	2	1
		5	4	3	2	1

Language Reframing Log
Power Words (cont)

Word	Frequency	Getting Settled—Phase II				
		Disruption				Connection
		5	4	3	2	1
		5	4	3	2	1
		5	4	3	2	1
		5	4	3	2	1
Intend, Plan		5	4	3	2	1
		5	4	3	2	1
		5	4	3	2	1
		5	4	3	2	1
		5	4	3	2	1
		5	4	3	2	1
		5	4	3	2	1
		5	4	3	2	1
		5	4	3	2	1
		5	4	3	2	1
Will		5	4	3	2	1
		5	4	3	2	1
		5	4	3	2	1
		5	4	3	2	1
		5	4	3	2	1
		5	4	3	2	1

Language Reframing Log
Power Words (cont)

Word	Frequency	Moving Forward—Phase III				
		Disruption				Connection
Intend, Plan		5	4	3	2	1
		5	4	3	2	1
		5	4	3	2	1
		5	4	3	2	1
		5	4	3	2	1
		5	4	3	2	1
		5	4	3	2	1
		5	4	3	2	1
		5	4	3	2	1
		5	4	3	2	1
Will		5	4	3	2	1
		5	4	3	2	1
		5	4	3	2	1
		5	4	3	2	1
		5	4	3	2	1
		5	4	3	2	1
		5	4	3	2	1
		5	4	3	2	1
		5	4	3	2	1
		5	4	3	2	1

Language Reframing Log
Power Words (cont)

Word	Frequency	Getting Started—Phase I				
		Disruption				Connection
		5	4	3	2	1
		5	4	3	2	1
		5	4	3	2	1
		5	4	3	2	1
Just		5	4	3	2	1
		5	4	3	2	1
		5	4	3	2	1
		5	4	3	2	1
		5	4	3	2	1
		5	4	3	2	1
		5	4	3	2	1
		5	4	3	2	1
		5	4	3	2	1
		5	4	3	2	1
Exactly		5	4	3	2	1
		5	4	3	2	1
		5	4	3	2	1
		5	4	3	2	1
		5	4	3	2	1
		5	4	3	2	1

Language Reframing Log
Power Words (cont)

Word	Frequency	Getting Settled—Phase II				
		Disruption				Connection
		5	4	3	2	1
		5	4	3	2	1
		5	4	3	2	1
		5	4	3	2	1
Just		5	4	3	2	1
		5	4	3	2	1
		5	4	3	2	1
		5	4	3	2	1
		5	4	3	2	1
		5	4	3	2	1
		5	4	3	2	1
		5	4	3	2	1
		5	4	3	2	1
		5	4	3	2	1
Exactly		5	4	3	2	1
		5	4	3	2	1
		5	4	3	2	1
		5	4	3	2	1
		5	4	3	2	1
		5	4	3	2	1

Language Reframing Log
Power Words (cont)

Word	Frequency	Moving Forward—Phase III				
		Disruption				Connection
Just		5	4	3	2	1
		5	4	3	2	1
		5	4	3	2	1
		5	4	3	2	1
		5	4	3	2	1
		5	4	3	2	1
		5	4	3	2	1
		5	4	3	2	1
		5	4	3	2	1
		5	4	3	2	1
Exactly		5	4	3	2	1
		5	4	3	2	1
		5	4	3	2	1
		5	4	3	2	1
		5	4	3	2	1
		5	4	3	2	1
		5	4	3	2	1
		5	4	3	2	1
		5	4	3	2	1
		5	4	3	2	1

Language Reframing Log
Power Words (cont)

Word	Frequency	Getting Started—Phase I				
		Disruption				Connection
		5	4	3	2	1
		5	4	3	2	1
		5	4	3	2	1
		5	4	3	2	1
No		5	4	3	2	1
		5	4	3	2	1
		5	4	3	2	1
		5	4	3	2	1
		5	4	3	2	1
		5	4	3	2	1
		5	4	3	2	1
		5	4	3	2	1
		5	4	3	2	1
		5	4	3	2	1
Not Yet		5	4	3	2	1
		5	4	3	2	1
		5	4	3	2	1
		5	4	3	2	1
		5	4	3	2	1
		5	4	3	2	1

184

Language Reframing Log
Power Words (cont)

Word	Frequency	Getting Settled—Phase II				
		Disruption				Connection
No		5	4	3	2	1
		5	4	3	2	1
		5	4	3	2	1
		5	4	3	2	1
		5	4	3	2	1
		5	4	3	2	1
		5	4	3	2	1
		5	4	3	2	1
		5	4	3	2	1
		5	4	3	2	1
Not Yet		5	4	3	2	1
		5	4	3	2	1
		5	4	3	2	1
		5	4	3	2	1
		5	4	3	2	1
		5	4	3	2	1
		5	4	3	2	1
		5	4	3	2	1
		5	4	3	2	1
		5	4	3	2	1

Language Reframing Log
Power Words (cont)

Word	Frequency	Moving Forward—Phase III				
		Disruption				Connection
		5	4	3	2	1
		5	4	3	2	1
		5	4	3	2	1
		5	4	3	2	1
No		5	4	3	2	1
		5	4	3	2	1
		5	4	3	2	1
		5	4	3	2	1
		5	4	3	2	1
		5	4	3	2	1
		5	4	3	2	1
		5	4	3	2	1
		5	4	3	2	1
		5	4	3	2	1
Not Yet		5	4	3	2	1
		5	4	3	2	1
		5	4	3	2	1
		5	4	3	2	1
		5	4	3	2	1
		5	4	3	2	1

186

Language Reframing Log
Power Words (cont)

Word	Frequency	Getting Started—Phase I				
		Disruption				Connection
Resolution		5	4	3	2	1
		5	4	3	2	1
		5	4	3	2	1
		5	4	3	2	1
		5	4	3	2	1
		5	4	3	2	1
		5	4	3	2	1
		5	4	3	2	1
		5	4	3	2	1
		5	4	3	2	1
Commitment		5	4	3	2	1
		5	4	3	2	1
		5	4	3	2	1
		5	4	3	2	1
		5	4	3	2	1
		5	4	3	2	1
		5	4	3	2	1
		5	4	3	2	1
		5	4	3	2	1
		5	4	3	2	1

Language Reframing Log
Power Words (cont)

Word	Frequency	Getting Settled—Phase II				
		Disruption				Connection
Resolution		5	4	3	2	1
		5	4	3	2	1
		5	4	3	2	1
		5	4	3	2	1
		5	4	3	2	1
		5	4	3	2	1
		5	4	3	2	1
		5	4	3	2	1
		5	4	3	2	1
		5	4	3	2	1
Commitment		5	4	3	2	1
		5	4	3	2	1
		5	4	3	2	1
		5	4	3	2	1
		5	4	3	2	1
		5	4	3	2	1
		5	4	3	2	1
		5	4	3	2	1
		5	4	3	2	1
		5	4	3	2	1

Language Reframing Log
Power Words (cont)

Word	Frequency	Moving Forward—Phase III				
		Disruption				Connection
Resolution		5	4	3	2	1
		5	4	3	2	1
		5	4	3	2	1
		5	4	3	2	1
		5	4	3	2	1
		5	4	3	2	1
		5	4	3	2	1
		5	4	3	2	1
		5	4	3	2	1
		5	4	3	2	1
Commitment		5	4	3	2	1
		5	4	3	2	1
		5	4	3	2	1
		5	4	3	2	1
		5	4	3	2	1
		5	4	3	2	1
		5	4	3	2	1
		5	4	3	2	1
		5	4	3	2	1
		5	4	3	2	1

Language Reframing Log
Power Words (cont)

Word	Frequency	Getting Started—Phase I				
		Disruption				Connection
To, At		5	4	3	2	1
		5	4	3	2	1
		5	4	3	2	1
		5	4	3	2	1
		5	4	3	2	1
		5	4	3	2	1
		5	4	3	2	1
		5	4	3	2	1
		5	4	3	2	1
		5	4	3	2	1
With		5	4	3	2	1
		5	4	3	2	1
		5	4	3	2	1
		5	4	3	2	1
		5	4	3	2	1
		5	4	3	2	1
		5	4	3	2	1
		5	4	3	2	1
		5	4	3	2	1
		5	4	3	2	1

Language Reframing Log
Power Words (cont)

Word	Frequency	Getting Settled—Phase II				
		Disruption				Connection
		5	4	3	2	1
		5	4	3	2	1
		5	4	3	2	1
		5	4	3	2	1
To, At		5	4	3	2	1
		5	4	3	2	1
		5	4	3	2	1
		5	4	3	2	1
		5	4	3	2	1
		5	4	3	2	1
		5	4	3	2	1
		5	4	3	2	1
		5	4	3	2	1
		5	4	3	2	1
With		5	4	3	2	1
		5	4	3	2	1
		5	4	3	2	1
		5	4	3	2	1
		5	4	3	2	1
		5	4	3	2	1

Language Reframing Log
Power Words (cont)

Word	Frequency	Moving Forward—Phase III				
		Disruption				Connection
		5	4	3	2	1
		5	4	3	2	1
		5	4	3	2	1
		5	4	3	2	1
To, At		5	4	3	2	1
		5	4	3	2	1
		5	4	3	2	1
		5	4	3	2	1
		5	4	3	2	1
		5	4	3	2	1
		5	4	3	2	1
		5	4	3	2	1
		5	4	3	2	1
		5	4	3	2	1
With		5	4	3	2	1
		5	4	3	2	1
		5	4	3	2	1
		5	4	3	2	1
		5	4	3	2	1
		5	4	3	2	1

Language Reframing Log
Power Words (cont)

Word	Frequency	Getting Started—Phase I				
		Disruption				Connection
		5	4	3	2	1
		5	4	3	2	1
		5	4	3	2	1
		5	4	3	2	1
Why		5	4	3	2	1
		5	4	3	2	1
		5	4	3	2	1
		5	4	3	2	1
		5	4	3	2	1
		5	4	3	2	1
		5	4	3	2	1
		5	4	3	2	1
		5	4	3	2	1
		5	4	3	2	1
How, What		5	4	3	2	1
		5	4	3	2	1
		5	4	3	2	1
		5	4	3	2	1
		5	4	3	2	1
		5	4	3	2	1

Language Reframing Log
Power Words (cont)

Word	Frequency	Getting Settled—Phase II				
		Disruption				Connection
		5	4	3	2	1
		5	4	3	2	1
		5	4	3	2	1
		5	4	3	2	1
Why		5	4	3	2	1
		5	4	3	2	1
		5	4	3	2	1
		5	4	3	2	1
		5	4	3	2	1
		5	4	3	2	1
		5	4	3	2	1
		5	4	3	2	1
		5	4	3	2	1
		5	4	3	2	1
How, What		5	4	3	2	1
		5	4	3	2	1
		5	4	3	2	1
		5	4	3	2	1
		5	4	3	2	1
		5	4	3	2	1

Language Reframing Log
Power Words (cont)

Word	Frequency	Moving Forward—Phase III				
		Disruption				Connection
		5	4	3	2	1
		5	4	3	2	1
		5	4	3	2	1
		5	4	3	2	1
Why		5	4	3	2	1
		5	4	3	2	1
		5	4	3	2	1
		5	4	3	2	1
		5	4	3	2	1
		5	4	3	2	1
		5	4	3	2	1
		5	4	3	2	1
		5	4	3	2	1
		5	4	3	2	1
How, What		5	4	3	2	1
		5	4	3	2	1
		5	4	3	2	1
		5	4	3	2	1
		5	4	3	2	1
		5	4	3	2	1

Language Reframing Log
Swing Words and Phrases

Word	Frequency	Getting Started—Phase I				
		Disruption				Connection
Get Over, Around		5	4	3	2	1
		5	4	3	2	1
		5	4	3	2	1
		5	4	3	2	1
		5	4	3	2	1
		5	4	3	2	1
		5	4	3	2	1
		5	4	3	2	1
		5	4	3	2	1
		5	4	3	2	1
Get Through		5	4	3	2	1
		5	4	3	2	1
		5	4	3	2	1
		5	4	3	2	1
		5	4	3	2	1
		5	4	3	2	1
		5	4	3	2	1
		5	4	3	2	1
		5	4	3	2	1
		5	4	3	2	1

Language Reframing Log
Swing Words and Phrases (cont)

Word	Frequency	Getting Settled—Phase II				
		Disruption				Connection
		5	4	3	2	1
		5	4	3	2	1
		5	4	3	2	1
		5	4	3	2	1
Get Over, Around		5	4	3	2	1
		5	4	3	2	1
		5	4	3	2	1
		5	4	3	2	1
		5	4	3	2	1
		5	4	3	2	1
		5	4	3	2	1
		5	4	3	2	1
		5	4	3	2	1
		5	4	3	2	1
Get Through		5	4	3	2	1
		5	4	3	2	1
		5	4	3	2	1
		5	4	3	2	1
		5	4	3	2	1
		5	4	3	2	1

Language Reframing Log
Swing Words and Phrases (cont)

		Moving Forward—Phase III				
Word	Frequency	Disruption				Connection
Get Over, Around		5	4	3	2	1
		5	4	3	2	1
		5	4	3	2	1
		5	4	3	2	1
		5	4	3	2	1
		5	4	3	2	1
		5	4	3	2	1
		5	4	3	2	1
		5	4	3	2	1
		5	4	3	2	1
Get Through		5	4	3	2	1
		5	4	3	2	1
		5	4	3	2	1
		5	4	3	2	1
		5	4	3	2	1
		5	4	3	2	1
		5	4	3	2	1
		5	4	3	2	1
		5	4	3	2	1
		5	4	3	2	1

Language Reframing Log
Swing Words and Phrases (cont)

Word	Frequency	Getting Started—Phase I				
		Disruption				Connection
		5	4	3	2	1
		5	4	3	2	1
		5	4	3	2	1
		5	4	3	2	1
Hanging In		5	4	3	2	1
		5	4	3	2	1
		5	4	3	2	1
		5	4	3	2	1
		5	4	3	2	1
		5	4	3	2	1
		5	4	3	2	1
		5	4	3	2	1
		5	4	3	2	1
		5	4	3	2	1
Staying With		5	4	3	2	1
		5	4	3	2	1
		5	4	3	2	1
		5	4	3	2	1
		5	4	3	2	1
		5	4	3	2	1

199

Language Reframing Log
Swing Words and Phrases (cont)

Word	Frequency	Getting Settled—Phase II				
		Disruption				Connection
		5	4	3	2	1
		5	4	3	2	1
		5	4	3	2	1
		5	4	3	2	1
Hanging In		5	4	3	2	1
		5	4	3	2	1
		5	4	3	2	1
		5	4	3	2	1
		5	4	3	2	1
		5	4	3	2	1
		5	4	3	2	1
		5	4	3	2	1
		5	4	3	2	1
		5	4	3	2	1
Staying With		5	4	3	2	1
		5	4	3	2	1
		5	4	3	2	1
		5	4	3	2	1
		5	4	3	2	1
		5	4	3	2	1

Language Reframing Log
Swing Words and Phrases (cont)

Word	Frequency	Moving Forward—Phase III				
		Disruption				Connection
		5	4	3	2	1
		5	4	3	2	1
		5	4	3	2	1
		5	4	3	2	1
Hanging In		5	4	3	2	1
		5	4	3	2	1
		5	4	3	2	1
		5	4	3	2	1
		5	4	3	2	1
		5	4	3	2	1
		5	4	3	2	1
		5	4	3	2	1
		5	4	3	2	1
		5	4	3	2	1
Staying With		5	4	3	2	1
		5	4	3	2	1
		5	4	3	2	1
		5	4	3	2	1
		5	4	3	2	1
		5	4	3	2	1

Business

Word	Frequency	Getting Started—Phase I				
		Disruption				Connection
		5	4	3	2	1
		5	4	3	2	1
		5	4	3	2	1
		5	4	3	2	1
Hope		5	4	3	2	1
		5	4	3	2	1
		5	4	3	2	1
		5	4	3	2	1
		5	4	3	2	1
		5	4	3	2	1
		5	4	3	2	1
		5	4	3	2	1
		5	4	3	2	1
		5	4	3	2	1
Trust, Expect		5	4	3	2	1
		5	4	3	2	1
		5	4	3	2	1
		5	4	3	2	1
		5	4	3	2	1
		5	4	3	2	1

Language Reframing Log

Swing Words and Phrases (cont)

Business

	Getting Settled—Phase II					
Word	Frequency	Disruption				Connection
		5	4	3	2	1
		5	4	3	2	1
		5	4	3	2	1
		5	4	3	2	1
Hope		5	4	3	2	1
		5	4	3	2	1
		5	4	3	2	1
		5	4	3	2	1
		5	4	3	2	1
		5	4	3	2	1
		5	4	3	2	1
		5	4	3	2	1
		5	4	3	2	1
		5	4	3	2	1
Trust, Expect		5	4	3	2	1
		5	4	3	2	1
		5	4	3	2	1
		5	4	3	2	1
		5	4	3	2	1
		5	4	3	2	1

Language Reframing Log
Swing Words and Phrases (cont)

Business

Word	Frequency	Moving Forward—Phase III				
		Disruption				Connection
Hope		5	4	3	2	1
		5	4	3	2	1
		5	4	3	2	1
		5	4	3	2	1
		5	4	3	2	1
		5	4	3	2	1
		5	4	3	2	1
		5	4	3	2	1
		5	4	3	2	1
		5	4	3	2	1
Trust, Expect		5	4	3	2	1
		5	4	3	2	1
		5	4	3	2	1
		5	4	3	2	1
		5	4	3	2	1
		5	4	3	2	1
		5	4	3	2	1
		5	4	3	2	1
		5	4	3	2	1
		5	4	3	2	1

Language Reframing Log
Swing Words and Phrases (cont)

Personal

Word	Frequency	Getting Started—Phase I				
		Disruption				Connection
Trust, Expect		5	4	3	2	1
		5	4	3	2	1
		5	4	3	2	1
		5	4	3	2	1
		5	4	3	2	1
		5	4	3	2	1
		5	4	3	2	1
		5	4	3	2	1
		5	4	3	2	1
		5	4	3	2	1
Hope		5	4	3	2	1
		5	4	3	2	1
		5	4	3	2	1
		5	4	3	2	1
		5	4	3	2	1
		5	4	3	2	1
		5	4	3	2	1
		5	4	3	2	1
		5	4	3	2	1
		5	4	3	2	1

Language Reframing Log
Swing Words and Phrases (cont)

Personal

Word	Frequency	Getting Settled—Phase II				
		Disruption				Connection
		5	4	3	2	1
		5	4	3	2	1
		5	4	3	2	1
		5	4	3	2	1
Trust, Expect		5	4	3	2	1
		5	4	3	2	1
		5	4	3	2	1
		5	4	3	2	1
		5	4	3	2	1
		5	4	3	2	1
		5	4	3	2	1
		5	4	3	2	1
		5	4	3	2	1
		5	4	3	2	1
Hope		5	4	3	2	1
		5	4	3	2	1
		5	4	3	2	1
		5	4	3	2	1
		5	4	3	2	1
		5	4	3	2	1

Language Reframing Log
Swing Words and Phrases (cont)

Personal

Word	Frequency	Moving Forward—Phase III				
		Disruption				Connection
		5	4	3	2	1
		5	4	3	2	1
		5	4	3	2	1
		5	4	3	2	1
Trust, Expect		5	4	3	2	1
		5	4	3	2	1
		5	4	3	2	1
		5	4	3	2	1
		5	4	3	2	1
		5	4	3	2	1
		5	4	3	2	1
		5	4	3	2	1
		5	4	3	2	1
		5	4	3	2	1
Hope		5	4	3	2	1
		5	4	3	2	1
		5	4	3	2	1
		5	4	3	2	1
		5	4	3	2	1
		5	4	3	2	1

Language Reframing Log
Swing Words and Phrases (cont)

Sales/Personal

Word	Frequency	Getting Started—Phase I				
		Disruption				Connection
		5	4	3	2	1
		5	4	3	2	1
		5	4	3	2	1
		5	4	3	2	1
Need		5	4	3	2	1
		5	4	3	2	1
		5	4	3	2	1
		5	4	3	2	1
		5	4	3	2	1
		5	4	3	2	1
		5	4	3	2	1
		5	4	3	2	1
		5	4	3	2	1
		5	4	3	2	1
Want		5	4	3	2	1
		5	4	3	2	1
		5	4	3	2	1
		5	4	3	2	1
		5	4	3	2	1
		5	4	3	2	1

Language Reframing Log
Swing Words and Phrases (cont)

Sales/Personal

Word	Frequency	Disruption				Connection
		\<Getting Settled—Phase II\>				
		5	4	3	2	1
		5	4	3	2	1
		5	4	3	2	1
		5	4	3	2	1
Need		5	4	3	2	1
		5	4	3	2	1
		5	4	3	2	1
		5	4	3	2	1
		5	4	3	2	1
		5	4	3	2	1
		5	4	3	2	1
		5	4	3	2	1
		5	4	3	2	1
		5	4	3	2	1
Want		5	4	3	2	1
		5	4	3	2	1
		5	4	3	2	1
		5	4	3	2	1
		5	4	3	2	1
		5	4	3	2	1

Language Reframing Log
Swing Words and Phrases (cont)

Sales/Personal

Word	Frequency	Moving Forward—Phase III				
		Disruption				Connection
		5	4	3	2	1
		5	4	3	2	1
		5	4	3	2	1
		5	4	3	2	1
Need		5	4	3	2	1
		5	4	3	2	1
		5	4	3	2	1
		5	4	3	2	1
		5	4	3	2	1
		5	4	3	2	1
		5	4	3	2	1
		5	4	3	2	1
		5	4	3	2	1
		5	4	3	2	1
Want		5	4	3	2	1
		5	4	3	2	1
		5	4	3	2	1
		5	4	3	2	1
		5	4	3	2	1
		5	4	3	2	1

Language Reframing Log

Swing Words and Phrases (cont)

Management

	Getting Started—Phase I					
Word	Frequency	Disruption				Connection
Want		5	4	3	2	1
		5	4	3	2	1
		5	4	3	2	1
		5	4	3	2	1
		5	4	3	2	1
		5	4	3	2	1
		5	4	3	2	1
		5	4	3	2	1
		5	4	3	2	1
		5	4	3	2	1
Need		5	4	3	2	1
		5	4	3	2	1
		5	4	3	2	1
		5	4	3	2	1
		5	4	3	2	1
		5	4	3	2	1
		5	4	3	2	1
		5	4	3	2	1
		5	4	3	2	1
		5	4	3	2	1

Language Reframing Log
Swing Words and Phrases (cont)

Management

		Getting Settled—Phase II				
Word	Frequency	Disruption				Connection
Want		5	4	3	2	1
		5	4	3	2	1
		5	4	3	2	1
		5	4	3	2	1
		5	4	3	2	1
		5	4	3	2	1
		5	4	3	2	1
		5	4	3	2	1
		5	4	3	2	1
		5	4	3	2	1
Need		5	4	3	2	1
		5	4	3	2	1
		5	4	3	2	1
		5	4	3	2	1
		5	4	3	2	1
		5	4	3	2	1
		5	4	3	2	1
		5	4	3	2	1
		5	4	3	2	1
		5	4	3	2	1

Language Reframing Log
Swing Words and Phrases (cont)

Management

Word	Frequency	Moving Forward—Phase III				
		Disruption				Connection
Want		5	4	3	2	1
		5	4	3	2	1
		5	4	3	2	1
		5	4	3	2	1
		5	4	3	2	1
		5	4	3	2	1
		5	4	3	2	1
		5	4	3	2	1
		5	4	3	2	1
		5	4	3	2	1
Need		5	4	3	2	1
		5	4	3	2	1
		5	4	3	2	1
		5	4	3	2	1
		5	4	3	2	1
		5	4	3	2	1
		5	4	3	2	1
		5	4	3	2	1
		5	4	3	2	1
		5	4	3	2	1

Language Reframing Log
Swing Words and Phrases (cont)

Word	Frequency	Getting Started—Phase I				
		Disruption				Connection
		5	4	3	2	1
		5	4	3	2	1
		5	4	3	2	1
		5	4	3	2	1
Not Bad		5	4	3	2	1
		5	4	3	2	1
		5	4	3	2	1
		5	4	3	2	1
		5	4	3	2	1
		5	4	3	2	1
		5	4	3	2	1
		5	4	3	2	1
		5	4	3	2	1
		5	4	3	2	1
Pretty Good		5	4	3	2	1
		5	4	3	2	1
		5	4	3	2	1
		5	4	3	2	1
		5	4	3	2	1
		5	4	3	2	1

Language Reframing Log
Swing Words and Phrases (cont)

Word	Frequency	Getting Settled—Phase II				
		Disruption				Connection
Not Bad		5	4	3	2	1
		5	4	3	2	1
		5	4	3	2	1
		5	4	3	2	1
		5	4	3	2	1
		5	4	3	2	1
		5	4	3	2	1
		5	4	3	2	1
		5	4	3	2	1
		5	4	3	2	1
Pretty Good		5	4	3	2	1
		5	4	3	2	1
		5	4	3	2	1
		5	4	3	2	1
		5	4	3	2	1
		5	4	3	2	1
		5	4	3	2	1
		5	4	3	2	1
		5	4	3	2	1
		5	4	3	2	1

Language Reframing Log
Swing Words and Phrases (cont)

Word	Frequency	Moving Forward—Phase III				
		Disruption				Connection
Not Bad		5	4	3	2	1
		5	4	3	2	1
		5	4	3	2	1
		5	4	3	2	1
		5	4	3	2	1
		5	4	3	2	1
		5	4	3	2	1
		5	4	3	2	1
		5	4	3	2	1
		5	4	3	2	1
Pretty Good		5	4	3	2	1
		5	4	3	2	1
		5	4	3	2	1
		5	4	3	2	1
		5	4	3	2	1
		5	4	3	2	1
		5	4	3	2	1
		5	4	3	2	1
		5	4	3	2	1
		5	4	3	2	1

216

Language Reframing Log
Swing Words and Phrases (cont)

Word	Frequency	Getting Started—Phase I				
		Disruption				Connection
Think, Feel, Believe, Know		5	4	3	2	1
		5	4	3	2	1
		5	4	3	2	1
		5	4	3	2	1
		5	4	3	2	1
		5	4	3	2	1
		5	4	3	2	1
		5	4	3	2	1
		5	4	3	2	1
		5	4	3	2	1
None of the choices		5	4	3	2	1
		5	4	3	2	1
		5	4	3	2	1
		5	4	3	2	1
		5	4	3	2	1
		5	4	3	2	1
		5	4	3	2	1
		5	4	3	2	1
		5	4	3	2	1
		5	4	3	2	1

Language Reframing Log
Swing Words and Phrases (cont)

		Getting Settled—Phase II				
Word	Frequency	Disruption				Connection
Think, Feel, Believe, Know		5	4	3	2	1
		5	4	3	2	1
		5	4	3	2	1
		5	4	3	2	1
		5	4	3	2	1
		5	4	3	2	1
		5	4	3	2	1
		5	4	3	2	1
		5	4	3	2	1
		5	4	3	2	1
None of the choices		5	4	3	2	1
		5	4	3	2	1
		5	4	3	2	1
		5	4	3	2	1
		5	4	3	2	1
		5	4	3	2	1
		5	4	3	2	1
		5	4	3	2	1
		5	4	3	2	1
		5	4	3	2	1

Language Reframing Log
Swing Words and Phrases (cont)

Word	Frequency	Moving Forward—Phase III				
		Disruption				Connection
Think, Feel, Believe, Know		5	4	3	2	1
		5	4	3	2	1
		5	4	3	2	1
		5	4	3	2	1
		5	4	3	2	1
		5	4	3	2	1
		5	4	3	2	1
		5	4	3	2	1
		5	4	3	2	1
		5	4	3	2	1
None of the choices		5	4	3	2	1
		5	4	3	2	1
		5	4	3	2	1
		5	4	3	2	1
		5	4	3	2	1
		5	4	3	2	1
		5	4	3	2	1
		5	4	3	2	1
		5	4	3	2	1
		5	4	3	2	1

Language Reframing Log
Throwaway Words

Word	Getting Started—Phase I	
	Experience Using	Experience Omitting
Interesting		
Nice		

Language Reframing Log
Throwaway Words (cont)

Word	Getting Settled—Phase II	
	Experience Using	Experience Omitting
Interesting		
Nice		

Language Reframing Log
Throwaway Words (cont)

Word	Moving Forward—Phase III	
	Experience Using	Experience Omitting
Interesting		
Nice		

Language Reframing Log
Throwaway Words (cont)

	Getting Started—Phase I	
Word	Experience Using	Experience Omitting
Should		
Could		

Language Reframing Log
Throwaway Words (cont)

	Getting Settled—Phase II	
Word	Experience Using	Experience Omitting
Should		
Could		

Language Reframing Log
Throwaway Words (cont)

Word	Moving Forward—Phase III	
	Experience Using	Experience Omitting
Should		
Could		

Language Reframing Log
Throwaway Words (cont)

Word	Getting Started—Phase I	
	Experience Using	Experience Omitting
Would		
Must		

Language Reframing Log
Throwaway Words (cont)

Word	Getting Settled—Phase II	
	Experience Using	Experience Omitting
Would		
Must		

Language Reframing Log
Throwaway Words (cont)

	Moving Forward—Phase III	
Word	Experience Using	Experience Omitting
Would		
Must		

Language Reframing Log
Throwaway Words (cont)

Word	Getting Started—Phase I	
	Experience Using	Experience Omitting
Try		

Language Reframing Log
Throwaway Words (cont)

	Getting Settled—Phase II	
Word	Experience Using	Experience Omitting
Try		

Language Reframing Log
Throwaway Words (cont)

Word	Moving Forward—Phase III	
	Experience Using	Experience Omitting
Try		

Language Reframing Log
Throwaway Words (cont)

Word	Frequency	Getting Started—Phase I				
		Disruption				Connection
		5	4	3	2	1
		5	4	3	2	1
		5	4	3	2	1
		5	4	3	2	1
Try		5	4	3	2	1
		5	4	3	2	1
		5	4	3	2	1
		5	4	3	2	1
		5	4	3	2	1
		5	4	3	2	1
		5	4	3	2	1
		5	4	3	2	1
Attempt,		5	4	3	2	1
Experiment,						
Explore,		5	4	3	2	1
Play,		5	4	3	2	1
Practice,						
Sample,		5	4	3	2	1
Test,		5	4	3	2	1
Work		5	4	3	2	1
		5	4	3	2	1
		5	4	3	2	1

Language Reframing Log
Throwaway Words (cont)

Word	Frequency	Getting Settled—Phase II				
		Disruption				Connection
		5	4	3	2	1
		5	4	3	2	1
		5	4	3	2	1
		5	4	3	2	1
Try		5	4	3	2	1
		5	4	3	2	1
		5	4	3	2	1
		5	4	3	2	1
		5	4	3	2	1
		5	4	3	2	1
		5	4	3	2	1
		5	4	3	2	1
Attempt,		5	4	3	2	1
Experiment,		5	4	3	2	1
Explore,		5	4	3	2	1
Play,		5	4	3	2	1
Practice,		5	4	3	2	1
Sample,		5	4	3	2	1
Test,		5	4	3	2	1
Work		5	4	3	2	1
		5	4	3	2	1

Language Reframing Log
Throwaway Words (cont)

Word	Frequency	Moving Forward—Phase III				
		Disruption				Connection
		5	4	3	2	1
		5	4	3	2	1
		5	4	3	2	1
		5	4	3	2	1
Try		5	4	3	2	1
		5	4	3	2	1
		5	4	3	2	1
		5	4	3	2	1
		5	4	3	2	1
		5	4	3	2	1
		5	4	3	2	1
		5	4	3	2	1
Attempt, Experiment, Explore, Play, Practice, Sample, Test, Work		5	4	3	2	1
		5	4	3	2	1
		5	4	3	2	1
		5	4	3	2	1
		5	4	3	2	1
		5	4	3	2	1
		5	4	3	2	1

Summary

isualizing the choices available in Action Based Communication on a scale, as in Figure 12 on the next page, illustrates the difference between creating a connection and causing a disruption.

What did you experience as a result of doing the exercises? How did the context affect your experience?

If your shoulders dropped and turned inward and if your chin was down hiding your neck, you are more likely to cause a disruption. Maintaining the Language Reframing Log will help you straighten up, lift your chin, and reduce the number of disruptions caused. Weigh the results of the exercises.

If you were aware that your shoulders were straight and your chin was up, revealing your neck, you are more likely to create a connection.

Connection	Disruption
And	But
Will	Intend, Plan
Exactly	Just
Not Yet	No
Commitment	Resolution
With	To, At
How, What	Why
Get Through	Get Over, Around
Staying With	Hanging In
Trust, Expect	Hope
(sales/business)	(sales/business)
Hope	Trust, Expect
(personal)	(personal)
Want (personal)	Need (personal)
Need	Want
(management)	(management)
Pretty Good	Not Bad
None of the	Think, Feel, Believe,
choices	Know
~~Interesting~~	Interesting
~~Nice~~	Nice
Willing, Want	Should, Could,
	Would, Must
~~Try~~	Try

Figure 12: Connection—Lighter than Disruption

Choose *Action Based Communication*
Experience the Joy of Connection

Appendix: Supporting Words Catalog

ollowing is a catalog of other words that play a crucial role in supporting communication and creating a connection. Working with these principles myself helped me through the period of uncertainty that was the genesis for Action Based Communication.

You can use the Supporting Words Catalog as a source to guide your communication and connection, both with yourself and with others.

Supporting Words Catalog

Quality	Meaning
Abundance	Enough or an overflow of the tangible and intangible
Acceptance	Working with a situation, individual, yourself as it is in the moment, without judgment
Authenticity	Genuine, real, reliable so that you are clear about your core; saves energy, making connecting easier
Balance	Equal distribution across mental, physical, emotional states
Belief	An unproven conviction in a Grand Architect or Spirit Master, in whatever form; provides an ongoing connection
Breath	An exchange of air; literally life support. If you find that you are stuck (as illustrated on p. 161), stop and take a few seconds to breathe deeply in and out four times. This breathing regenerates the flow of oxygen to the brain.

Quality	Meaning
Celebration	Recognition in some physical way of an achievement (e.g., jumping, doing a jig, or patting yourself on the back when you've completed something; getting away from the office as a team to revel in a product launch)
Compassion	Capacity to be with or join with another person's experience with care and concern and a willingness to act on that person's behalf
Courage	Acting in accordance with your beliefs keeps you connected to yourself; putting yourself in uncomfortable situations allows for expanded connections
Delight	Pleasure, satisfaction as a result of some exchange, connection
Direction	A clear line of thought or purpose; moving along the line creates connection
Discovery	Gaining knowledge to create a connection with something new
Encouragement	Boosting confidence, cheering for, and supporting someone, which almost immediately creates connection

Quality	Meaning
Enthusiasm	Maintaining a lively interest for an activity or idea; creates connection similarly to encouragement
Ethics	Moral guidance/principles
Flexibility	The ability for a mind or body to move or bend easily
Forgiveness	Ability to let go of resentment; pardoning yourself or others who you feel wronged you
Friendliness	A spirit (indescribable) that invites others to connect
Generosity	Giving emotionally, mentally, and materially
Grace	A manner of elegance, beauty, simplicity
Gratitude	Heartfelt (vs. perfunctory) thanks
Honesty	Forthright; preserves energy for creating connections
Humility	Modest, unpretentious; also preserves energy for creating connections
Humor	Amusing, comedic anecdotes; stories that create a smile
Jazz	Energy, liveliness

Quality	Meaning
Journey	Progression from one place, phase to another; creates a connection
Joy	A dancing and singing heart
Laughter	Merriment, mirth, lightening and lifting; release of air
Learning	Acquisition of knowledge
Love	Profound tenderness, affection
Magic	Desired outcomes achieved through the seemingly supernatural or unknown
Miracles	Extraordinary events that surpass what we know, feel, see, smell
Mystery	An inexplicable quality or character that can draw people in
Participation	Sharing yourself; offering in a way that contributes to a stronger outcome
Passion	Powerful emotions, interest, belief
Patience	Willingness to wait, slow down
Rest	A cessation of activity that allows time to connect with yourself and then others
Risk	Exploration of new, different ways of being, doing

Quality	Meaning
Ritual	Repetition of a practice; provides support and comfort
Safety	Protection; a basic requirement for any physical structure and human relationship
Silence	Absence of sound; allows for taking in thoughts, conversations
Space	Expanse in which "everything" occurs, exists (e.g., vertebrae need space to move, which literally support us)
Values	Ideals, customs
Variety	Different forms, qualities, types
Vision	Idea, fantasy, image, dream, inspiration that is not yet a reality
Way	Manner, plan, progress, opening
Wisdom	Enlightenment, insight, understanding
Wonder	Admiration, amazement, astonishment, awe
Zeal	Eagerness, fervor
Zest	Essence, hearty enjoyment
Zing	Liveliness, vitality

References

Bandler, Richard and Grinder, John. *Frogs into PRINCES: Neurolinguistic Programming* . Edited by John O. Stevens. Moab, Utah: Real People Press, 1979

Bandler, Richard and Grinder, John. *The Structure of Magic I—A Book About Language & Therapy*. Palo Alto: Science and Behavior Books, Inc., 1975

Buzan, Tony. *Use Both Sides Of Your Brain*. New York: E.P. Dutton, 1974

Carnegie, Dale. *How to Stop Worrying and Start Living*. New York: Simon and Schuster, 1944

Ekman, Paul. *Emotions Revealed*. New York: Henry Holt and Company, 2003

Goleman, Daniel. *Emotional Intelligence*. New York: Bantam Books, 1995

Grinder, John and Bandler, Richard. *The Structure of Magic II: A Book About Communication and Change*. Palo Alto: Science and Behavior Books, Inc., 1976

Hall, Edward T. *The Silent Language*, New York: Anchor Books, 1990

Jaworski, Joseph. *Synchronicity: The Inner Path of Leadership*. San Francisco, Berret-Hoehler, 1996.

Kegan, Robert and Lahey, Lisa Laskow. *How the Way We Talk Can Change the Way We Work*. San Francisco: Jossey-Bass, 2001

Linden, Anné with Perutz, Kathrin. *Mindworks*. New York: Berkley Books, 1997

McGinn, Colin. *The Character of Mind: An Introduction to the Philosophy of Mind*, 2nd ed. Oxford, England: Oxford University Press, 1997

McGinty, Sarah Myers Ph.D. *Power Talk: Using Language to Build Authority and Influence*. New York: Warner Books, 2001

O'Connor, Joseph and Seymour, John. *Introducing NLP* 2nd ed. London, England: Thorsons, 1995

Pinker, Steven. *The Language Instinct: How the Mind Creates Language*. New York: HarperPerennial, 1994

Russell, Peter. *The Brain Book*. New York: E.P. Dutton, 1979

Schlain, Leonard. *The Alphabet Versus the Goddess: The Conflict Between Word and Image*. New York: Penguin Putnam, 1998

Schwartz, Jeffrey M. M.D., and Begley, Sharon. *The Mind and the Brain: Neuroplasticity and the Power of Mental Force*. New York: Harper Collins, 2002

Scott, Susan. *Fierce Conversations: Achieving Success at Work & in Life, One Conversation at a Time*. New York: Viking, 2002

Searle, John R. *Consciousness and Language*, New York: Cambridge University Press, 2002

Searle, John R. *Speech Acts: An Essay in the Philosophy of Language*. New York: Cambridge University Press, 1990

Stone, Douglas; Patton, Bruce; and Heen, Sheila. *Difficult Conversations: How to Discuss What Matters Most*. New York: Viking, The Penguin Group, 1999

About the Author

Renée Barnow has enjoyed a life-long fascination with language, especially words, and the role they play in creating connections. She was first published in a local daily newspaper at age 8. A few years later, as the literal "new kid on the block," she started a street newsletter. Involved in the formal communication business for more than 30 years, Renée's career has evolved from working at a static level (writing technical, instructional, marketing, and business materials) to working at a dynamic level (consulting with and coaching individuals and teams and facilitating groups).

Renée is the founder and principal of Rightline, a company that provides coaching and consulting services. She invites readers to share their experiences using material from Action Based Communication with her at renee@right-line.com and to visit her websites: www.right-line.com and www.actionbasedcommunication.com.

Renée lives in Washington, DC.